D1392001

A PARENT'S GUIDE TO
ANOREXIA AND BULIMIA

A PARENT'S GUIDE TO

ANOREXIA
AND
BULIMIA

UNDERSTANDING
AND HELPING
SELF-STARVERS
AND
BINGE/PURGERS

KATHERINE BYRNE

WITH AN AFTERWORD BY
BERNARD MACKLER, PH.D.

SCHOCKEN BOOKS / NEW YORK

First published by Schocken Books 1987
5   4   3   2   1   87   88   89   99

Library of Congress Cataloging-in-Publication Data
Byrne, Katherine.
    A parent's guide to anorexia and bulimia.
    Bibliography: p.
    Includes index.
    1. Anorexia nervosa—Popular works. 2. Bulimia—
Popular works. I. Title. [DNLM: 1. Anorexia Nervosa—
popular works. 2. Bulimia—popular works. WM 175 B995p]
RC552.A5B97   1987   616.85'2   87-4878

Design by Cassandra J. Pappas
Manufactured in the United States of America
ISBN 0–8052–4032–2

The author is an award-winning writer of books and articles on health and personality. She chose to use the assumed name Katherine Byrne in respect for the privacy of her daughter, who is recovering from "anorexia nervosa," or self-starvation.

TO MY DAUGHTERS

CONTENTS

INTRODUCTION

Your child has suddenly decided to become thinner than any human being can be and still expect to live. You didn't even realize it was happening. You pick her up at the end of summer camp. She's wearing shorts and your stomach heaves when you see her bones sticking out. What do you do? Where do you look for advice? Who can help?

As recently as five or six years ago, the disorders known as anorexia nervosa and bulimia were virtually unknown to the general public and not very familiar to psychologists and psychiatrists. Correct diagnoses were rarely made, victims often went untreated, and the treatment that was available was not necessarily effective. There was practically no literature on the subject outside of highly abstruse scientific journals. *The Golden Cage* by the pioneering specialist in eating disorders, Hilde Bruch, was the only book available that was written in language understandable to the layperson. Unfortunately, it suffered from a fault common to nearly all early writing on the subject: an excessive preoccupation with the role of the mother in the development of obsessive dieting.

Since then, eating disorders have become "fad" diseases, covered ad nauseum in the popular press. Psychiatrists and psychologists have begun to specialize in their diagnosis and treatment, and solid research is now beginning to enlighten the scientific community and the general public about the causes and nature of these illnesses. Indeed, some excellent books have been written about them. Most of the books are of three types: scientifically oriented books written by psychologists, psychiatrists, or physicians and intended for the professional audience; books written by nonscientists and intended largely for the victims of these disorders; and books written by the victims themselves. The focus in all of these books is chiefly on the victim. One rarely finds detailed descriptions of the everyday conflicts, problems, and pain entailed in this illness for the parents of these children; nor does one easily find specific advice to parents on how to deal with these difficulties in a way that also helps the afflicted children.

Parents struggling through volume after volume of specialized literature often find themselves confused by the contradictory explanations of the causes of eating disorders and by the descriptions of a bewildering variety of therapeutic approaches. Most important, parents find that many of the scientific texts tend to describe the disorder as resulting from parental failures. This only exacerbates the guilt they already suffer. When not featured as the culprits in the case, parents are virtually ignored.

In the therapeutic process, too, parents are often left out to a great degree. Some therapists feel they should not even talk to the parents, in the belief that the child needs to be able to speak with total freedom to her therapist, trusting that the therapist will not spill any of her secrets to anyone. Even when the parents are involved with the therapy, the focus is still almost exclusively on the victim. In short, very little attention is paid to the difficulties and sufferings of the parents. Of course, the child with an eating disorder is certainly the one most in need of help. But if the child is to be helped effectively, the parents must be informed, supported, reassured. They also need to know what the child needs from them. These needs vary from one person to another since, despite popular notions, every person who suffers from an eating disorder is an individual, distinct and different from all other victims except for the disorder they have in common. Needs also vary from time to time in the same person. It is vital for parents to know when to take it easy and when to be tough, how to offer support without being intrusive, how to respect the child's needs without neglecting their own. It is also essential to know what to do about such daily problems as a child's refusal to eat with the family, or a child's insistence on doing all the cooking, refusal to go to school, shoplifting, theft, or hiding food under her bed. Some psychologists recommend that families should be involved in therapy—or at least informed about it:

> The family can be mobilized to be more supportive if provided information about the patient's illness. As their understanding of the patient's symptoms and problems becomes more accurate, there will be a reduction in their own feelings of guilt over the possible cause of the condition, or anger at the patient for not being able to control the symptoms through the exercise of will. Further, the family can be guided in responding supportively, without attacking the patient. Patient and family may then be free to work together toward agreed upon goals.[1]

In addition, parents who are uninformed may sabotage the therapy by unwitting errors in their handling of a situation. Furthermore, while therapy is essential, it is not enough. A visit to the therapist, after all, amounts to only 45 minutes once or twice a week. Parents, on the other hand, are there 18 hours a day, 365 days a year.

My entire professional career—the past twenty-five years—has been devoted to writing about medical and emotional health. The last five of those years have also been occupied with struggling through the frightening and bewildering experience of seeing my child starve herself to near death, with desperate efforts to help her recover, and with moments of terrifying helplessness. During that time I regularly sat and listened to the unbearable stories of other parents at support group meetings, and was sustained and steadied by their encouragement and sympathy. Their frequent expressions of a wish for a practical guidebook that would help them help their children to survive—even triumph over—this almost indescribable experience was what first prompted me to try to combine my years of professional experience as a writer with my personal experience as a parent.

There are some things this book will do, and some things it will not. First, it will avoid as much as possible the term "anorexia." I don't like it.

I don't like it because it's an ugly-sounding word to describe something fundamentally touching and sad. And "anorectic" is an ugly-sounding thing to call somebody whose deepest and most urgent need is to be thought beautiful. I also don't like it because "anorexia" means "absence of appetite," and except in certain specific situations, people with this condition do not lose their appetites. They are *hungry, hungry, hungry.* This term is additionally inaccurate as a description of this condition because it is derived from the Greek "an," meaning "without," and "orexis," meaning "longing." Girls with this condition, however, are not without longing. They are filled with longing, consumed by longing, desperate with longing.

In fact, I don't like it simply because it's Greek. Foreign terms for things, especially things medical or psychological, imply either mystery or matters too intellectually or scientifically exotic for ordinary folk. Anorexia nervosa is a complicated condition but it can be talked about in ordinary language.

For these reasons, I will use the term "self-starver," because it is a straightforward word that also emphasizes that the starver is doing it to herself. But since self-starver is too long a term to be used as often as it needs to be in writing about it, it will often be shortened to "starver." Similarly, instead of bulimarexia or bulimia I will use "binge eating/purging," or just "binge eating." (It is understood that practically all binge eating is followed by purging of one kind or another.)

By using simple terms, I hope to eliminate some of the mystery associated with the scientific terms. Self-starvers use a lot of magic and ritual. Certain foods must be placed in a specific spot on a plate, the bathroom scale must be precisely lined up with a certain row of tiles, the day must be programmed not just to the hour but to the minute. It is my hope to demystify these acts and the illness that generates them.

The basic premise of this book is that self-starvation and binge/purging are terribly inefficient and self-destructive attempts to solve the problems of adolescence, and that parents can help their children to find more positive and healthy problem-solving methods. People who starve themselves are usually trying to cope with, or avoid, some of the complex challenges of the transition from childhood to maturity, but they lack effective coping tactics. For various reasons, they discover self-starvation as a "solution." Unhappily, for the starver this method feels like a real solution because in many ways—at least in the beginning—*it works.* In fact, it accomplishes wonders that might be envied by (and has much in common with) the toddler who sits down on the pavement and screams his head off to make mother buy him candy. Self-starvation gets attention, it brings the family into line, and it makes the starver the one who calls the tune. It allows the starver to escape many of the responsibilities and burdens of growing up. Best of all, this strategy provides the starver with an unassailable identity. People may disagree about one girl's good looks, another's singing voice, or a third's cheerleading style, but nobody can disagree about whether a girl who is five foot three and weighs eighty pounds is *thin.*

Eventually the starver becomes aware that something is wrong, that this ideal solution to her problems is not so ideal.

In her eyes, she has become beautiful and special and ought to be popular and happy. But she doesn't have enough energy to enjoy it. In weather that is barely cool she's too cold to go outside for any length of time. Her hair doesn't shine so much anymore, her lips and fingers may be blue. And what she begins to see in the faces of those she cares about is not admiration and wonder but pity, pain, and fear. She is bedeviled by guilt: guilt for what she is doing to her family, guilt each time she "slips" from her rigid diet, each time she is "imperfect." At this point, ideally, she would say to herself, "This isn't working as well as I thought." For many reasons, however, she can't do that. One of the most important is that *the illness becomes the starver's identity,* her whole life's focus. She cannot give it up without something to replace it, or her life will be totally empty and without a center. She herself will be nothing. This is understandably terrifying, and parents must fully accept and grasp this basic fact if they are to guide their child to health.

One important goal of those who try to help the self-starver is to enable her to recognize the nature of her behavior as bad problem-solving, and to support her in the process of learning better problem-solving tactics. Looking at the disorder this way is actually very encouraging. Thinking of it as a complex, mysterious, unfathomable emotional illness, on the other hand, is frightening, confusing, and tends to discourage efforts to deal with it. If the condition is seen as poor problem-solving, it can be corrected by good problem-solving. It can be thought of not as something that has to be cured, but something the starver can solve herself with appropriate help.

This way, the self-starver is free of shame or embarrassment. After all, we all make mistakes. The person who recognizes and accepts mistakes and attempts to correct them has reason to be proud, not ashamed or guilty. This is a difficult point to make to a self-starver, because the perfectionist inside her cannot imagine that it is acceptable to make a mistake and to admit it. It is one of the parents' major chores to convince the starver (by word, but even more important by act) that perfection is an unattainable goal and its pursuit a frustrating and self-defeating activity.

This book will provide practical suggestions for parents in handling this task as well as the many others that must be undertaken to help the self-starver recover. This book will *not*, however, tell parents how to cure their child. This is not a job for which parents are equipped. Whatever one's opinion may be of the value or effectiveness of psychotherapy in other kinds of emotional problems, the record almost incontrovertibly supports the statement that people with eating disorders must have professional help. Happily, professional help of the right kind is often highly effective.

This book is designed to help parents cope with the little-known but sometimes overwhelming difficulties of living with someone who has an eating disorder. It is designed to help parents be of maximum support and minimum hindrance while their child is receiving professional therapy. I also hope to help parents recognize that they are not "the only ones," that other children besides their own behave in equally bizarre ways, that they are not "the worst parents in the world," at fault for this terrible suffering.

Throughout the book, the pronoun "her" will be used in referring to someone with an eating disorder. This is for convenience. It is not intended to overlook the fact that eating disorders do occur in males. (Indeed, they occur with increasing frequency, largely because of increasing emphasis in our society on fitness and athletic accomplishment.) Similarly, the starver will usually be spoken of as a child or adolescent. Self-starvation does sometimes begin in the late twenties or even thirties, but in the overwhelming majority of cases, onset is somewhere around puberty. The older starver and the binge eater present special practical problems for those who are trying to help, but essentially the underlying problem-solving difficulties are of a similar order. Throughout the book, therefore, suggestions for dealing with "the starver" may be considered to apply equally well to the binge eater, except where specifically stated otherwise.

Because self-starvation and binge/purging are so widely known today, it has seemed redundant to provide great detail about the symptoms and the psychological and physiological effects of the disorder, except to provide some guidance to those parents who may at the moment merely suspect that their child is developing an eating disorder.

These are the things to watch for:

Fad dieting. The child who suddenly begins limiting food intake only to, say, grapefruit and spinach, papayas, or saltines, or who severely restricts her diet to one group of foods—such as only protein or carbohydrates—should be watched with an extremely cautious eye. Most often, in the normal young person or teen-ager, such diets are quickly dropped because they are boring, inconvenient, and leave the dieter hungry most of the time. Any fad diet maintained for more than a few weeks at any one time is unhealthy and may be a sign of an impending eating disorder.

Long-term dieting. Even if the child is on a "sensible" diet, a diet balanced in nutritional components but restricted in calories, parents should be concerned if the diet is severely low-caloric, or if she continues on it for a long period.

Behavior changes. Moodiness, impatience, rudeness, and similar unpleasant behavior sometimes accompany dieting even in otherwise normal people. Hunger and the metabolic/chemical changes that go with reduced food intake often make people cranky. These are often just brief flare-ups and can be seen to occur in a pattern, usually just before a meal, when the dieter is hungriest and blood sugar is lowest. With eating disorders, these behavior changes are more pervasive. If a child who has previously been honest and open begins to be secretive, if she has always been gregarious but now begins spending hours alone behind a closed door, if she loses interest in friends, favorite sports, or activities—all of these may only represent ordinary teenage unpredictability. However, coupled with changes in eating patterns, such behavior may have a more serious significance.

Excessive exercising. One of the things people find so striking about self-starvation is that a person whose food intake seems to provide barely sufficient energy for picking up a pencil nevertheless can spend hours jogging, cycling, doing calisthenics, swimming, playing soccer, and running (never walking) up and down stairs dozens of times. Exercise is essential to health and absolutely necessary in weight control. Carried to an extreme it is a sign of abnormality.

Weight loss without dieting. If a child or young woman is eating normally or even more than normally but loses weight, parents should suspect that she is somehow purging herself of food. The index of suspicion goes up if she leaves the table immediately after eating and stays in the bathroom for a while. This is a strong clue to the binge/purge syndrome. Laxative abuse or the repeated use of ipecac to induce vomiting may be harder to detect, but any hint that the child is taking either one calls for immediate action. Laxative abuse and ipecac purge can kill suddenly and with little or even no warning.

Depression. This most often comes after the eating disorder is well established, and in the ideal situation, the problem should have been recognized and dealt with before it reaches this stage. When a child has been exhibiting any or all of the other signs of an eating disorder and also appears depressed or withdrawn, seems to lack ambition, or makes comments about having no future or feeling "empty," parents should act promptly to get help. Suicidal remarks, however mild, should be taken with great seriousness. Direct suicide (as opposed to starving oneself to death) is rare in eating disorders, but it does happen. Depression even without suicidal undertones is never to be taken lightly, and in eating disorders it carries the added disadvantage of making it more difficult to get the child motivated to seek therapy.

These signs, or any other subtle or overt behavioral changes in a child that lead to parental uneasiness, should not be brushed away as "just a phase she's going through." The "phase" can stretch into years of misery.

Helping a son or daughter who has an eating disorder may require more patience, firmness, love, wisdom, and strength than any parent can possibly be expected to have. Yet parent after parent has discovered that they have enough of all these— and more.

Many starvers have described their recovery as a "discovery," a learning process from which they have emerged stronger and more confident, with more self-knowledge and understanding than they would have had if they never had suffered from this condition. What is less widely known is that parents, too, go through the same process of discovery. Many a parent has emerged from the experience having undergone change, a learning process, even a growing up. It is, however, difficult to see or appreciate this consoling aspect of the situation while in the midst of it. When a child hovers on the edge of starvation, or when the battle of wills between parent and child reaches intolerable intensity, it would be a rare parent indeed who could imagine that anyone would ever benefit. It is a common misconception that suffering has an inevitably humanizing effect. On the contrary, suffering often desensitizes people, makes them callous, indifferent or cynical, or even brutalizes them. There is nothing inherent in the struggle with eating disorders that insures the participants will emerge as "better people." But there is a tremendous potential for it. It is a comforting thing to keep in mind when the night seems longest and darkest.

The other thing that is useful to keep in mind, when you feel you can no longer go on, when you have completely run out of strength or hope, is that thousands of other parents have felt the same way but have summoned (from who knows where) one more bit of strength, just enough to rejoin the struggle and carry on again. People who never before thought of themselves as strong have found iron in their spines; people who have always thought themselves impatient have found themselves bearing silently and with stoicism things they recognized could not be changed—yet.

Now I want to issue a warning—or perhaps it is a reassurance. There are many direct recommendations about what parents can or should do in this book. The recommendations are not given lightly or without great thought. They have many years of painful experience behind them. But I am concerned as I try to relieve parents' burden of guilt that I may unwittingly add to it by giving recommendations that, in fact, no human being could follow precisely and in every detail. Let me tell a story.

I had my hair cut by a new stylist during the writing of this book. I hated the result and felt humiliated that I had handed myself over entirely to someone else's whim about how to cut my hair. I was furious at the haircutter's insensitivity and lack of skill. By the time I reached home, I had worked myself into a state of fury. All of this I dumped on my self-starving daughter after she greeted me with, "What happened to your hair?"

All the time I was venting my frustration, anger, and dismay, the back of my mind was telling me something. "This is exactly the wrong thing to do. You are contradicting all the other things you are trying to persuade your daughter of. You're reinforcing her belief that appearances are all-important. You're telling her that you have so little confidence in yourself that if something is wrong with your hair, you feel like you're down the drain."

And in fact, that voice inside me was right. All the messages I was sending were wrong ones for my daughter. But I am no more a perfect human being than I am a perfect mother. Like anyone else, I get priorities mixed up, I get upset over trivialities, I am easily susceptible to insult—real or imagined—and I am no more capable of doing the right thing every time than anybody else. So my behavior on that occasion might have had a negative effect on my daughter. On balance, however, I think that to have stifled my feelings, pretended not to be upset, wouldn't exactly have had a positive effect. My daughter would have sensed something was wrong and been hurt because I wouldn't confide it to her.

In dealing with a self-starving child, parents can sometimes become so obsessed with trying to do the right thing that they become incapable of doing anything at all. One must, of course, try to do one's best—but one must not try to be perfect. That is one of the starver's big problems. Among many valuable things I have learned in the course of my daughter's suffering and my own is not to be too hard on myself. It is a lesson for all parents to learn and to try to help their children learn as well.

A PARENT'S GUIDE TO
ANOREXIA AND BULIMIA

ONE

HOW DID THIS HAPPEN?

What many parents of self-starvers feel at first is total bewilderment. Later, they feel sickening guilt. One of the first things parents often ask themselves is, "Why didn't we notice sooner what was happening?" Frequently, it is not the parents themselves who first notice that their daughter's thinness has reached an alarming stage. It is quite often first pointed out by someone outside the family. Parents commonly rebuke themselves (if somebody doesn't do it for them) for being so blind or indifferent that somebody else had to tell them that their daughter looks terrible.

Parents should let themselves off the hook over this. There is good reason why the close family of a child who is getting just a little thinner every day might well be the last to notice.

"Often it is an aunt or other distant relative who visits two or three times a year and who hasn't seen the girl for several months who is so shaken by the amount of weight her niece has lost that she galvanizes the parents into action by her transparently horrified reaction at her niece's appearance," say Jill Welbourne and Joan Purgold, therapists at the University of

Bristol.[1] Parents often get bad press on this issue, and it is usually unfair and undeserved.

"People who say 'How could they ignore how thin their daughter has become?' forget that human perceptions make comparisons and do not perceive absolute levels of measurement," the therapists explain, citing the experiment in which a person submerges the left hand in cold water and the right hand in hot water. After a minute, if both hands are then put into lukewarm water, the left hand will feel hot and the right one cold, even though the temperature of the water is the same for both hands. "In other words, what you perceive is determined by your previous experience. The parents find that their child has not changed much since yesterday. The aunt finds that her niece is very different from how she was two months ago. Both are right—but they have had different experiences."[2]

The next more serious source of bafflement and guilt does not come from the child's physical condition, but from her emotional state and behavior. Suddenly and without warning, it seems, there is a stranger in the family, a baffling creature who, with unruffled calm and quiet deliberation, is turning herself into a thing of skin and bones. Her personality undergoes frightening changes. Her behavior is inexplicable and intolerable. The parents do not understand her feelings or actions at all, and are desperate for some knowledge about causes. One of the most urgent questions parents ask when they first attend a parent-support meeting is, "Why did our daughter get this way?"

Nobody can answer this question specifically and it probably does not matter. For the most part, recovery depends on the victim grappling with the present: confronting her behavior and its consequences, and deciding that she no longer wants to live her life this way. There are interesting and, no doubt, valid theories about the origins of this disease. There are also individual and family-life patterns that contribute to the development of eating disorders, and the recognition of these patterns, leading to some healthy change, might work in favor of the starver. But it is extremely difficult—usually impossible—to discover the specific cause of an eating disorder in any individual. It is more important for parents to understand what is going on in the family at the moment, and what their child is thinking and feeling. This is not so difficult. Self-starvers and binge eaters are all distinct individuals, but their feelings have a commonality. First, let me describe in simplest terms what she is thinking and feeling:

"I am worthless, a nobody. I don't have anything special about me. Nobody pays any attention to me.

"I can never live up to my parents' expectations of me. I'm always to blame.

"I am helpless, not in control of my life. I can't control the way people treat me. I can't control the way my face looks or my straight hair. I can't control my future. What on earth can I control?

"I can control what I eat.

"I want the world to notice me and admire me. The world thinks thin is good. If I am thin, the world will think I'm good. If I am thinner than anybody else, I will be *somebody*. If I'm not thin, I'm nothing.

"All these feelings are too overwhelming. I'm hungry. I'm scared."

On the face of it, these are obviously irrational, unhealthy feelings. Of all the aberrations of thinking and behavior common among adolescents, these seem the most bizarre, the most unreasonable. One recovered self-starver has said that, in fact, "it's a very logical illness. What could be more rational for someone who can't cope with life than to literally fade away from it?" There are a great many theories about how eating disorders develop. Some suggest that a major factor in self-starvation is the changing roles of women and the contradictions they confront. Today

> women are expected to be beautiful, smart and well groomed, and to devote a great deal of time to their personal appearance even while competing in business and the professions. They must have a career and yet be romantic, tender and sweet, and in marriage play the part of the ideal wife *cum* mistress and *cum* mother who puts away her hard-earned diplomas to . . . perform menial chores. It is quite obvious that the conflict between so many unreconcilable demands on her time, in a world where the male spirit of competition and productivity reigns supreme, exposes the modern woman to a terrible social ordeal.[3]

Noting the sharp increase in eating disorders in recent years, Dr. John Sours feels it is apparent that our society and culture have changed in the last two decades. While it would be difficult to make a direct connection between these changes and the development of eating disorders, people do respond to societal forces, often in dramatic ways. According to Dr. Sours, "societal and cultural institutions are no longer trusted, societal and group ego-ideals do not mitigate a sense of insecurity; relationships are shallow and open to exploitation; narcissistic therapies have replaced religion in celebration of the self. . . . These factors and others blur the boundaries of the self, make people feel vulnerable to passivity, loss of control, and liable to intrusion, invasion, and control by vague, outside forces."[4] He sees a parallel between eating disorders and the recent mania for running and fitness, considering them "symptomatic of the changes in our society and the emergence of a prominent ego-style." Both running and food disorders "have captured the interest of the media, which, one suspects, may be responsible for the increased numbers in both the eating disorder and the sport."[5]

Another theory is that self-starvers diet excessively in order to evade the responsibilities of adulthood or to avoid confronting the nature and consequences of adult sexuality.

Many psychologists and psychiatrists today agree on the more basic principle that eating disorders arise in response to the challenge of adolescence, and that the choice of this inefficient way of meeting that challenge results from a complex interaction of individual personality and family dynamics in the framework of powerful social forces. Many of the factors in the development of adolescent eating disorders are, in fact, not specific to those disorders but are common to adolescents in general.

This is one of the reasons that it is so difficult to explain any specific case of self-starvation: the childhood history, family background and social pressures that influence a particular girl who has become a self-starver could be virtually identical to those of another girl who has not. Eating disorders can be viewed as part of a rather varied repertoire of inefficient or abnormal adjustments to the challenge of adolescence.

Adolescence could well be described as a period of intense hard labor. At perhaps no other stage in life are the challenges greater and the resources for dealing with them less well developed. The transition from childhood to adulthood in modern society is infinitely more difficult and laborious than the struggles of a snake to shed its old skin or of a butterfly to emerge from its hard-shelled cocoon. One self-starver spoke of "the mounting pressures that accumulated to such an extent in my teens that I developed anorexia as a refuge."

Among the most basic tasks the adolescent faces are forging an identity, dealing with emerging sexuality, separating from the family, and establishing relationships with peers. To these may be added some modern refinements: passing achievement tests, determining a career choice, getting accepted into a good college, coping with peer pressures regarding sexual behavior and drug or alcohol abuse, and trying to find one's way through today's confusion over gender roles. In all relatively affluent nations, especially in America, there is the added need to meet society's ubiquitous and unrealistic standards of bodily perfection, focused on thinness. This pressure is inescapable.

Every young person has to find his or her own way of meeting these challenges, and few do it perfectly. In fact, few teenagers have the competence and skills to meet the many challenges of maturity without trouble or pain. Those who seem to meet it best are those who bring to the struggle some sense of self-esteem and competence. The self-starver enters the battle with no such ally: low self-esteem is the one universally shared characteristic of starvers and binge eaters.

A. H. Crisp, the leading British specialist in eating disorders, has said that self-starving is only likely to arise "if less primitive and less self-destructive postures are unattainable. . . . At the stage at which anorexia develops, apparently other coping mechanisms are not available. Often the problem seems to be overwhelming and is not conceptualized or shared with others."[6]

Often, indeed, the problem arises just at the time when the teen-ager is becoming reluctant to talk about her intimate feelings and concerns with her parents or other close relatives, or at a time when parents or siblings who might have been helpful and supportive are themselves going through some form of anxiety or conflict. Parents may be going through the "midlife crisis" or may have reached that point at which marriages so often begin to weaken. A sibling who has been a good friend to the potential self-starver may not be available as a resource because he or she is confronting college, marriage, or parenthood.

The self-starver also may lack peer support or she may be unable to forge the peer relationships that are essential to the transition from family orientation to society orientation. Self-starvers often lack close friendships. If the self-starver manages to have any relationships at all, it is usually with only one person and it is often temporary. Her lack of self-esteem stands in the way of popularity and acceptance by "the crowd," and (in the vicious circle of problems typical of the self-starver) her lack of popularity increases her lack of self-esteem. Without resources in the family, among her peers, or within herself, the pre-starver looks around for another weapon: an artificial source of security and self-esteem.

The late Hilde Bruch, a pioneer in the study and treatment of eating disorders, reports: "Not one of the anorexic patients whom I have come to know over the years had set out to reach this state of pitiful emaciation. All they had wanted to achieve was to feel better about themselves. Since they had felt that 'being too fat' was the cause of their despair, they were determined to correct it. Whatever weight they reached in this struggle for self-respect and respect from others, it was 'not right' for giving them self-assurance, and so the downhill course continued."[7] One girl treated by Dr. Bruch had suffered all her life from feeling she was ugly. She began dieting, and eventually lowered her weight from 140 to 67 pounds. She explained that being fat was something she could do something about, but being ugly wasn't. She knew her skeleton-like appearance was hideous, but her argument was, "What if my weight went back to normal and I were still ugly, then what would I do?" At the same time, Bruch adds, "She knew that what was covered under the term 'ugly' applied as much to psychological attributes and to disappointment in her own achievements and behavior as to the physical evidence."[8]

In other words, the self-starver yearns for something to make her special, to counteract her feelings of unattractiveness or unworthiness. Eventually she will find this "something" in control of food. She may not be able to control her emerging and frightening sexual feelings, or the agonies of self-doubt and pain she feels from the inevitable teasing and criticism among teens, or any of the other conflicting and difficult needs and feelings of adolescence. She *can* control what she eats.

The discovery of self-starvation as a source of control and its resulting "specialness" most often begins with the beginning of the physical changes of early adolescence. It is a time when both boys and girls commonly suffer from what has been termed "dysmorphophobia"; that is, acute sensitivity about appearance or about specific parts of the body—to the point of being fearful about these things. Young people, for example, worry about the size or shape of their noses, the placement of their ears, their height.

First the starver-to-be interprets the rounding of the body in puberty as fatness. She is no different in this than virtually all other adolescent girls; it is a universal experience. Those girls not destined to become self-starvers, however, respond differently. They may, indeed, diet. However, they will either diet to their desired weight goal and stop, or they will diet for a time and give it up, only to diet again another day. Their sense of self does not depend utterly on their shape.

The starver-to-be, by contrast, may begin to diet in the same way as her friends, but in time there is a marked change in both her feelings and her dieting behavior. As the changes of puberty follow each other in their unstoppable pattern, she feels that terrible things *are being done to her.* These changes are imposed by some inexorable outer force. She does not identify them or accept them as being a part of her natural development, of her individual self, as coming from within her. She feels helpless to control these bodily changes. She may become highly superstitious, speak of herself as "a born loser," or begin talking about some form of higher power that "doesn't like me" or "is punishing me." The self-starver often adopts strange magic rituals designed to ward off this strange force that has taken control of her life: never leaving a room without touching the door three times with the forefinger, never going to bed without first turning the light on and off a specific number of times.

In a vain effort to achieve and maintain control, she continues to diet beyond the point where her "normal" friends would have quit, having reached their desired goal of attractiveness. She becomes "hooked" on the sense of achievement that losing weight gives her. Welbourne and Purgold say this seems to be the main reason why starvers continue to lose weight after they have reached their original target. "To stop losing weight and to stay at a stable (even though reduced) level is to deprive oneself of the sense of achievement; it is to lose the reassurance that the daily step on the bathroom scales can give."[9] At the same time, the step on the scale is a daily confrontation with the fear of gaining weight. "If the worst happens and an unintended weight gain occurs, the girl will then swing into her old pattern of weight restriction. The overwhelming probability is that she will overdo her efforts. A weight gain of two pounds usually produces a response which causes the girl to lose another seven. The lower weight now becomes the upper limit which must not be exceeded. To lose weight is comforting; weight gain has come to mean failure. She will suffer anything to avoid that outcome."[10]

The more she diets, the more she begins to suffer from desperate bouts of hunger, and the more preoccupied she becomes with food and eating—or rather, not eating. She also becomes obsessed with what others eat. Welbourne and Purgold quote the roommate of a self-starver as complaining that "she'd never come out to eat with us but when we came back to the flat we had to tell her about every mouthful we had eaten. When it was her turn to cook for the flat she got frantic if we looked as though we were not going to eat all she had cooked. . . . We had to go on and on until every mouthful had disappeared or she'd get so tense that life became impossible."[11]

Many parents also complain of their child's pressure on the eating behavior of others in the family. "We hear of brothers who have become seriously overweight through eating everything their anorexic sister has cooked for them. Parents entering their forties and fifties find their attempts to control the start of their own middle-age spread are blocked by their daughter's insistence that father should eat the last piece of lemon meringue pie and that mother can't possibly go without a cream cake (because then there would be one left over). Parents and husbands sometimes eat more than they want because they know that the starver will eat something, just so long as it is less than they eat. 'In order to get her on to survival rations we had to overeat,' said one rueful father."[12]

In time, she begins to "benefit" from the various secondary concomitants of excessive dieting. Her menstrual periods cease, or if they have not yet begun, she realizes that all her friends are menstruating but she is being "spared." She is pleased because menstruating is hateful to her both as a sign of maturity, which she wishes to avoid, and in itself. Starvers are often obsessive about body cleanliness and neatness and repulsed by certain natural bodily functions such as excretion and sex. They commonly describe their periods as messy, dirty, disgusting, and inconvenient.[13] (Menstruation has been shown to be directly related to a minimal body weight, below which menses are suppressed. In a remarkable study of self-starving and nonstarving school girls, A. H. Crisp has found that the starver's "ideal" body image is precisely that weight above which menstruation begins.[14] The starver, of course, has no idea of this connection, and it is not likely that this is a conscious motivation.)

There are other benefits. The starver's friends have begun to "notice" her. Her family has begun to pay her more attention and show more concern. She has not consciously planned this, but she cannot help noticing it and feeling gratified by it. "This self-starving has a lot to be said for it," her subconscious tells her. "I'm in charge. I can do this incredible thing that other people can't do: I can go without food."

There is, however, one terrible problem. She is hungry. She is sometimes so hungry it is frightening. It is so powerful, in fact, that she "knows" if she gives in to it she will be totally defeated by it. Self-starvers have a marked tendency to see everything as either black or white, good or bad, all or none. They cannot even imagine it is possible to eat in moderation.

The irony is that in order to control her appetite and to ignore the body's need for food, she starves herself to the point where her hunger forces her to be preoccupied with food and eating. She begins to doubt she can control her food intake any more than she has been able to control her other emotions, impulses, and conflicts. All the biological forces within her demand that she eat; the emotional forces insist that she forgo eating. It is this powerful conflict that contributes so much to her defensive, hostile, and tyrannical behavior in the family, especially as it relates to eating, meals, food-buying and cooking. As some therapists have pointed out, it may be precisely the increased hunger and faltering control that so dramatically intensifies her fear of becoming fat.

Of course, the modern teen-ager's definition of "fat" is unrecognizable to anyone born before the 1950s. When the mothers of most of today's self-starvers were themselves in their teens, the curves of puberty were not "fatness." They were the visible signs of one's progress into the wonderful, free, exciting, mysterious world of adulthood.

Today, many girls and young women find adulthood intimidating and frightening rather than exciting and mysterious. What is sex all about? they wonder. Their exposure to it in conversation, in the movies and on television, hardly paints an attractive picture: the ugly language of dirty sex is the daily coin of their peers' conversation. The exploitive, punishing nature of the sexual behavior of certain kinds of men is offered as entertainment far more than the loving and cherishing behavior of most mature men. Social attitudes toward sex seem to suggest that it is not a matter of choice; everybody does it, and those who do not are even more "out of it" than those who refuse to smoke pot or drink beer. In the 1980s, an even more sinister dimension has been added: the fear of AIDS. Even the nonstarving girl approaching sexual maturity and contemplating the possibility of sexual intimacy these days is frightened by the knowledge that AIDS can be transmitted heterosexually. And far too often, the person who transmits it doesn't even know he or she has been exposed. All these are added examples—to the mind of the self-starver—of her inherent lack of control over her own body and life.

As Crisp says:

> Cultural forces relevant to anorexia nervosa seem to me to have to do with the adolescent female's perception of the society she is entering in much broader terms than simply shape; namely, its degree of structure and limit setting through customs and institutions of a religious and secular kind, its values and its degree of caring set against her own emerging impulses, sense of competence and self-esteem, and the value system of the family from which she stems. In our present-day chaotic society, self-discipline has to take more extreme forms. It seems to me that anorexia nervosa is a biological solution to an existential problem in our modern society.[15]

In other words, the self-starver looks at the world and sees few rules or structures to guide her to an identity. Instead, the messages she receives from family and society are contradictory and intimidating. Sex is the thing to do; sex is violent, uncaring, ugly. Women should be attractive; thinness to the point of sexlessness is the goal of every self-respecting young woman. Women are liberated, free to be whatever they want to be; women are objects to be grabbed, used, and discarded. Women can do anything *they* want; women must be all things to all people.

Other contradictions are everywhere. Women's magazine covers alternate between glamorous photographs of ultraslim models and gorgeous full-color pictures of super-rich chocolate desserts. Articles on diet and fitness exhort women to have perfect bodies and promise them all the rewards of virtuous self-denial while advertisements describe certain foods as "wickedly" delicious, or tell the TV viewer that she "deserves a break today," consisting of cheeseburgers and fries.

It should be remembered that the victims of this disorder are not drawn evenly from society but are virtually all females. This is so for two major reasons. One is the traditional emphasis on the importance of a woman's appearance (as opposed to those attributes—character, intelligence, moral fiber, and talent—that largely govern people's attitudes toward men). The second is the conflicting societal signals a young woman receives today. In spite of the gains made in economic equality for women, these signals are still chiefly sexist—often severely so. Whatever victories the proponents of equality for women may claim, it is abundantly evident that a woman is first of all judged by the way she looks—in particular the way her body looks.

All these messages and influences are conflicting and confusing for all adolescents, but they are vastly more so for the self-starver, who is far more prone to rely on others for her self-evaluation than she is to find it within. Part of the world tells her that she is valuable for herself—for what she is or what she does. The other part of the world tells her that she is still an object to be *used* in various ways and to be judged. No wonder she feels trapped, without control, without identity.

TWO

THE TERROR
AND THE TYRANNY

The self-starver "has her back to the wall," says A. H. Crisp. "Within this context, she is often seen by others as being extremely manipulative and hysterical whilst her manner and moods are found unpredictable. Her rituals, her shoplifting, her alcoholism, her occasional depression, and her ecstacy through relief at successful control of her stance are likely to be misconstrued and are deeply puzzling and distressing to those around her."[1] This clinical description is often translated by the parents of self-starvers into the simple cry, "We can't stand it any more."

The victim of an eating disorder is often portrayed as compliant, well-behaved, always eager to please. This is not always the case. Some starvers have been described by their parents as having been difficult children even before their eating disorder began. In other cases, the description may have been accurate before the illness and it may also fit the starver's intentions during her illness. However, almost in spite of herself, the starver commonly becomes a domineering, demanding, temperamental person who extorts the family's obeisance to her needs.

Emotional and psychological pressures certainly contribute to such a transformation, but the physiological and neurological effects of starvation have a tremendous impact that is often overlooked or underestimated. "For the hungry person, culture, politics, family and friends are irrelevant; an interest in the welfare of others is impossible. Many starving anorectics fit this description. Despite frequent claims to the contrary, they are often ravenously hungry. They are also profoundly egocentric at very low weights. Although prior to the onset of anorexia nervosa, these patients were usually highly sensitive to cultural and family expectations, at their lowest weights they are frequently oblivious to the needs of those around them."[2]

One of the terrible aspects of the starving or binging/purging syndromes is that the victim is often out of control. Unable to solve her terrifying dilemma and feeling lost and helpless and beyond the reach of help, she tries desperately to get some kind of grip on her situation. Not knowing how to do this in healthy, effective ways, she uses ineffective strategies. These are often carryovers from infancy and childhood and are totally inappropriate to her current age and developmental stage. She may, for example, be uncomfortable about accompanying her parents to a family Thanksgiving dinner, but is incapable of confronting the issue, of discussing it with them and enlisting their understanding. Instead she adopts a childish tactic: she doesn't start getting dressed until the last minute, she dawdles and delays the family's departure. They, meanwhile, have no idea why she is doing this and can only fume with impatience and impotence. She herself doesn't really understand what she is doing. She does not know why she is engaging in behavior that is foreign to her true nature, baffling and hurtful to her parents, and self-defeating and intolerably guilt-producing to herself. Although she is actually struggling fiercely to save herself, her behavior seems bent on self-destruction. In her terrified search for love, approval, and identity, she seems to do those very things destined to alienate her from her family and provoke their anger, impatience, and disapproval. Some of the behavior is related to her chaotic feelings; some of it is her way of exercising the adolescent's normal rebelliousness. In the case of the child with an eating disorder, however, rebelliousness cannot take the form of direct disobedience or an overt deviation from the opinions and attitudes of her parents. The starver is too insecure and too guilt-prone to rebel overtly.

Her difficult behavior may begin rather simply, with the imposition of strictly limited menus and rigid eating schedules, but it inevitably extends farther and farther into other areas. She may expect the family to stop inviting people to dinner because she can't bear to eat in front of other people or to see others "stuffing themselves." She may also demand exclusive access to certain areas of the house where she can pursue her fanatic exercise regimen, or insist that television sets and radios be turned down to an inaudible point because semi-starvation has made her hearing painfully acute. She may pressure for a change in vacation plan because the current one does not allow her to pursue her obsessional rituals of eating, exercising, and weighing. She may say it is because she is "too fat" to be seen in a bathing suit—although she weighs 20 to 30 percent less than her ideal weight. Often, self-starvers will take possession of the bathroom scales and not allow anyone else to use them for fear of "throwing them off" in some way. The starver may forbid others to bring certain foods in the house, or not allow butter to be placed on the same refrigerator shelf with her low-fat cottage cheese. If she has the binge/purge form of the illness, she may hide food in her closets or under her bed, refusing to clean up and forbidding anyone else to come in to do it.

Other starvers become obsessively neat and may demand that the entire family meet their unrealistically fastidious standards. No magazine or pair of slippers or coffee cup may be left out of place for a moment. They may become equally, or even more, obsessed with personal hygiene and appearance, spending hours in the bathroom with the door locked and refusing to allow others to come in to get ready for school or work. The starver's sleep patterns are often abnormal. A working mother may sit up all night by her daughter's bed because the daughter suffers such severe night terrors she cannot bear to be left alone; or a working father's sleep may be disrupted by the sound of his daughter pacing the floor all night.

Often without realizing what is happening, adapting themselves bit by bit to individual inroads on their personal freedom and needs, the family discovers that previous habits and patterns have disappeared and all family life is directed by, and subservient to, the needs of the starver. The tyranny may even escalate to the point where the family's personal, social, and working lives are virtually destroyed. Siblings also suffer when parental attention and energy are consumed by coping with the ill child, and when family life becomes abnormally concentrated on the illness.

It is difficult to imagine how an otherwise normal family could allow such destructive behavior to continue. But like the starver herself, the families become tyrannized by fear. Parents acquiesce to demands and manipulations because they are terrified that resistance may precipitate more serious mental illness, death by starvation, or suicide. Ironically, their acquiescence only serves to provide the attention the starver so desperately needs, reinforces her notion that her parents do not have the strength or wisdom to resist her tyranny, and thus escalates her feelings of insecurity and her doubt of her parents' ability to help her. This behavior, then, only perpetuates the illness. It is, unfortunately, extraordinarily difficult for parents to be able to recognize this fact or to be firm about rules and standards of behavior for *all* members of the family when they are confronted by a hysterical, determined, pathetic seventy-five pounds of skin and bone.

One father, a highly placed executive accustomed to directing the activities of a large staff, described to a parents' self-help group how he often went out in the middle of the night searching for a grocery that was still open and that carried a particular brand of crackers, because his daughter suddenly wanted something to eat and only that kind of cracker would satisfy her. "I would come home exhausted and tense, unable to go back to sleep, because I couldn't believe I was actually doing this," he said. "But I couldn't help myself. I was afraid not to do it for her."

An older couple whose daughter had suffered from an eating disorder from ages fourteen to twenty-four described how, during her teen years, they used to go to her room to find she had disappeared. "She would climb out the window and go for long walks late at night," they said. Her reason for going out of the window and not the front door was that she was afraid her parents would stop her. "We never tried to tie her down or prevent her from going out," they said. "We just wanted to know where she was. Sometimes we would stay up all night waiting for her, scared to death of what might have happened to her."

Self-starvers' routines may become as rigid as marine boot-camp training. Some have their days scheduled not just by the hour but by the minute, and they will stick to these schedules no matter how they might interfere with the schedules or plans of other family members. Some starvers insist that dinner must be served precisely at six every evening—even if the mother has to work a little late and comes home tired and harassed. Dinner must be cooked immediately just the same. One starver's precisely controlled eating ritual required that she have a private snack at 4 P.M. Nobody else was allowed into the kitchen during the half-hour when she consumed this snack.

Starvers often want to control exactly what food is bought and when. Once the groceries are brought home, for example, they must be put in certain precise arrangements in the icebox or on the shelves. Parents who accept the starver's domination in this respect may find themselves desperately seeking to follow rules that are virtually impossible. For example, the starver may specify that no meat can be served. (Starvers are often extremely health- and nutrition-conscious as well as calorie-conscious.) They favor fresh, uncooked fruits and vegetables, avoid red meats, additives, preservatives, and artificial sweeteners. Some, however, go to the other extreme and live on diet colas. At the same time, the starver may insist that meals be low-caloric and that she cannot stand the smell of fish. Whoever does the cooking in the house is confronted with the necessity of either finding a suitable number of low-caloric chicken recipes or attempting to meet the family's protein requirements with such things as cheese, eggs, and legumes: excellent protein sources but very high in calories. Among the other unattractive alternatives are cooking one meal for the starver and a second meal for the rest of the family. Efforts to resist or even compromise on food issues may result in major confrontation. Some parents deal with their daughter's need for total dominance by offering her one shelf all her own in the icebox, or one cabinet of her own. Sometimes this works, but often the starver finds nothing acceptable short of total control over the family food supplies.

The starver often takes over not only the direction of the family meals but also the cooking and serving. Some become excellent cooks, serving up gourmet dinners, which they themselves refuse to eat but which they insist the family consume down to the last bite. One starver explained that she enjoyed watching others eat and that it gave her a great sense of pride to be able to deny her own hunger while others were "being pigs."

Hilde Bruch tells of a family that had been reluctant to admit that their brilliant, much admired daughter could be in need of treatment but finally sought help because her behavior was disrupting family life. She would get up early in the morning and make a huge breakfast, not allowing the younger children to go to school until they had eaten every morsel. Another girl would not let her parents go to bed until they had eaten all the cake and cookies she had baked after school. The girl's mother finally sought help because she herself was getting fat.[3]

Bruch points out that this obsessive preoccupation with food is not exclusively the behavior of the self-starver; it is also common to people who are starving involuntarily. People deprived of food because of food shortages often "toy" with their food or prepare what would ordinarily seem to be distasteful dishes. Political prisoners have reported that their limited meals were never eaten normally, but in great secrecy and with methods that would stretch the meal over the longest possible time. They spoke constantly about food, recipes, and fantasies of what they would eat when free.[4]

The physical effects of starvation include such visible symptoms as a skeletal appearance, anemia, dry skin, and a low body temperature, often accompanied by blue fingers and lips. There are also hidden neurological and endocrinological effects that have a powerful influence on behavior. It is important for parents and others close to the self-starver to understand that a large part of her intolerable behavior is rooted in her physical state. In other words, she cannot help behaving the way she does because her state of semistarvation is making her do it. For example, it was long thought that self-starvers were people with obsessive-compulsive personalities. But scientific studies have indicated that while some people were obsessive before they developed their eating disorders, many were not. The studies found that their obsessive behavior—carefully rearranging food on the plate, eating one bite of this, one bite of that, one bite of another in strict rotation, weighing themselves at precise times of the day, several times a day—was related directly to their physical state.[5]

Other disturbances in thinking and feeling that may result from starvation are the following:

Selective abstraction—reaching false conclusions based on one fact or detail while ignoring other factors or possibilities. For example, "Last night I ate everything on my plate even though I had decided ahead of time I wouldn't. I'm so weak."

Overgeneralization—assuming that one event constitutes a rule that will apply to other events that have nothing in common with it. "When I used to eat carbohydrates, I was fat. So I mustn't eat carbohydrates now, or I'll get fat."

Magnification—assigning far too much significance to the consequences of a given act. "Gaining five pounds would push me over the brink." Or, "I've gained two pounds; I can't go swimming because I will look horrible in a bathing suit."

All-or-none reasoning—thinking in extreme and absolute terms. "If I gain one pound, I'll gain a hundred. If I'm not in total control, I lose *all* control."

Personalization and self-reference—seeing everything, even impersonal events, as related to oneself, or overinterpreting events that are related to oneself. "Two people laughed and whispered something to each other as I walked by. They were probably saying that I'm fat."

Superstitious thinking—believing in a cause-effect relationship between unrelated events. "If I eat the meat before the vegetables, I will gain more weight."[6]

Starvers also become acutely sensitive to all sorts of external stimuli, such as noises or odors. One self-starver couldn't bear to have her father read the paper in the same room with her because he rattled the pages when he turned them. Others become hysterical over the loudness of a TV set or radio, even when it's turned on in the family room downstairs and the starver is upstairs in her own room.

Typical behavior related to the disordered thinking of semistarvation include such things as putting a tea kettle on the stove without any water in it, starting out for school or a doctor's appointment much too early, too late, or even on the wrong day. Mary Wazeter, a championship long-distance runner, whose life was nearly destroyed by starving and binge/ purging, has said, "I couldn't even watch TV, keep up my end of a conversation, or keep track of simple belongings like my room key and ID card. I'd arrive late for cross-country practice and consequently would have to run alone. Even worse, sometimes I'd wander off campus into the big city, Washington, D.C. and get hopelessly lost. It was terrifying—I no longer felt in control of my actions."[7]

An even worse consequence of the physical and neurological changes of starvation is depression. In Mary Wazeter's case this led to two suicide attempts, first by swallowing a variety of pills, then by a near fatal jump off a bridge onto ice 35 feet below. She survived the jump, but it left her paralyzed for life.

Any symptoms of disordered thinking, even the mildest, are reason enough for parents to take decisive action to get their child the physical and psychological help she needs. These symptoms are one of the reasons that most psychologists believe that some weight gain is necessary before psychological intervention can work. As long as the starver's thinking is distorted by her physical condition, she can hardly deal with the effort required for psychological recovery.

If her condition is allowed to persist untreated, the starver may become increasingly isolated from the world, refusing to go out, to see friends, to have any contact with society other than a robotic attendance at school or work. The starver's new behavior may also include alcoholism and theft—from parents or people for whom she works or babysits. The last hospitalization of a seventeen-year-old who had been in and out of hospitals over a period of several years was described by her father: "She climbed out of a window in the night and broke into a nearby home, where she raided the refrigerator and the liquor cabinet and made a mess in the kitchen. The owner caught her, called the police, and she was arrested." The father immediately offered to pay the homeowner for the stolen food and drink and for cleaning the kitchen, and appealed to him to drop the charges because of the girl's condition and the dangerous effect a trial could have on her. He refused. For months the father was in and out of court, repeating his appeals to the homeowner, running up large legal bills, and jeopardizing his own job because of the time and energy devoted to the effort. Eventually, through the intercession of a neighborhood priest, the homeowner relented and withdrew the charges. The girl was returned to the hospital, from which she again escaped within a few days.

For anyone who has not experienced the behavior of a victim of self-starving or binge/purging, these descriptions are hard to believe. Even harder to believe is that families allow such behavior to continue. Sometimes these patterns of starver tyranny continue for years. Asked how they could let such things happen or let them go on, most parents will explain that it happens bit by bit, one day at a time. Not understanding why they are happening and without guidance about how to deal with them, families usually find it easier to accommodate themselves to the behavior than to resist it.

Such acquiescence not only makes family life intolerable, it can also be extremely harmful to the starver. It seems to suggest approval or at least acceptance of the starver's behavior and does nothing to discourage it. Acquiescence, in other words, does not help the starver learn more efficient and acceptable ways of coping. It is, therefore, one of the forms of family behavior that parents must change.

In general, family dynamics play a crucial role in the way any young person develops and matures, and family behavior may need modifying. Hilde Bruch, for instance, says:

> If the family problems are not attended to, and parents are
> motivated by anger and anxiety in their dealings with the

anorexic patient, increasingly turbulent situations will develop with frantic mutual accusations. It is of course no easy situation: the anorexic girl can control the entire household with her petulant demands, refusal to eat or threats of suicide, and nothing is done to help her achieve inner security or true independence. It is not sufficient to advise the parents to show no interest in the youngster's eating or, the opposite, to instruct them to control her eating. It is important that the underlying patterns of interaction are recognized and that the family accept help in changing them. . . . When parents are well informed and not too defensive, they will make treatment arrangements on their own decision.[8]

Families who do get professional help usually become much better able to deal with their child. A great deal, however, depends on the kind of help they seek (see chapter 7 on kinds of therapy). If the child alone is in therapy, the parents may receive little or no guidance about their possible role in her recovery, about what they are supposed to do while she is trying to recover. This is one of several reasons why many families seek family therapy. For those not in family therapy, it is essential that some knowledge, advice, and support be available to the parents, either through separate therapy for either or both of them, or through parent support groups—preferably both.

Support groups can be particularly helpful because most of the parents who attend them have had considerable experience coping with self-starvers and have also learned a great deal from other parents in the group. Much of the knowledge and advice that can be gained from other parents could not even be learned from a therapist, since therapists themselves have never dealt with the day-to-day situation families must confront. A typical session in a group might go something as follows:

The leader opens the meeting by welcoming a new couple attending for the first time. She asks them if they want to tell the group about their problem.

"We just found out a month or so ago that our daughter, who is 17, has anorexia. She is seeing a therapist—we all went together once and she has been by herself three times. Her therapist said that after that one visit, we would not be involved in her sessions and that he would not discuss her with us any more, for the sake of her privacy and his need to develop a trusting relationship with her. So we've read every book and article we could get our hands on, but we're still confused and worried. We came here today because we thought maybe you people have the answers."

There are smiles around the table. "Do we?" one member asks. "Yes, we have some," says another. "First, tell us more about your daughter. How did you come to realize your daughter had anorexia? Did she talk to you about it? Did you have any trouble getting her to go for help? Who is her therapist?"

As the new parents talk, other members of the group occasionally interject a remark. "She's a terrific therapist. You made a good choice." "Do you have other children? How are they?"

And some answers do emerge. The mother wants to know what to do about her daughter never wanting to eat regular meals with the family. "Should I insist, or should I leave her alone? She wants to do all the grocery shopping. Should I let her?"

"Don't make an issue of eating with the family," a parent advises. "Try not to make an issue of anything having to do with food. Let the therapist deal with that. Avoid confrontations."

"You mean I should let her do *anything* she wants?"

"No, no," comes a chorus of objections. "You have to keep order in the family. Just don't make issues over food or eating or weight. The business of her wanting to eat alone will probably cure itself after she's been in therapy for a while."

"Can we ask her anything about what's going on in therapy?"

"That's tricky. Some girls resent anything that seems to be prying. Has your daughter been honest and open with you so far?"

The parents reply that their daughter willingly acknowledged that she had a problem when they finally realized it and confronted her with it.

In that case, the group agrees, it would be all right for the parents to open up possibilities for conversation about therapy, because anything they could learn would help them to support the therapist's efforts and avoid behavior or actions that might sabotage it.

"But don't ask her directly," one parent urges. "Show interest and let her take the initiative about discussing details. Say something like, 'I hope you had a good session today,' or even, 'You know, we'd like to learn anything you feel like telling us about your therapy. We'd like to cooperate and help.' "

There are, of course, no firm rules or step-by-step programs that are appropriate to every family of every starver. Parents and family dynamics differ as much as starvers differ, and how the family copes will depend a great deal on the parents' and the starver's personalities and their relationships and styles of coping before the starving began.

Psychotherapists say they are able to deal with the difficult behavior of self-starvers much more easily than parents simply because they are not emotionally involved. Parents are so enmeshed in their children's lives and care for their children so much that they cannot be objective or stand back and look clearly and coolly at what is happening. It is impossible—and fundamentally undesirable—for parents to have the objectivity of a paid professional therapist, but they can strive for some clearheadedness. The goal is to be emotionally warm and loving but intellectually one step removed. It is helpful to be able to separate the behavior from the person to some extent, to understand that it is the illness that produces the behavior. The child is the unwilling victim of her own chaotic feelings and needs.

Parents can best deal with the problem if their own relationship with each other is a good and trusting one. They can point out to each other kinds of behavior that are not working or are making things harder for their child—the kinds of things that are so much easier for another person to see than for the person doing them. But this can *only* be done if the parents are true partners, not if it turns into sniping or a power struggle. If the parents are capable of self-examination of themselves as individuals and as marriage partners, if they can recognize that there may be fundamental flaws in the relationship, then they may be able to mend these flaws, especially if they seek counseling. If quarreling and conflict have been common before the child developed the eating disorder, or if they become so afterward, the causes and solutions *must* be sought diligently. A family in conflict is an unhealthy family, even for children without the added burden of an eating disorder. Furthermore, it is quite common for parents in such a situation to make their daughter the fulcrum of their battles, to enlist her on one side or the other, or to create triangles with her as the apex. These are all negative influences on a child who is trying to find her identity apart from her family. *No child can find a solution to her problems in the midst of a family that cannot solve its own.*

Parents should be aware that even after their child has entered counseling, there will be periods of great difficulty. The very slowness of the process is disheartening. There will be times when little weight has been gained, her eating habits are still bizarre, and her behavior seems almost unchanged. Families can become very discouraged. "They lack reassurance and wonder whether they should have done—perhaps even now ought to do—something different. Their despondency communicates itself to the anorexic who in turn reflects, in therapy, the general household gloom. Every domestic event seems to be inconvenient or a downright disaster. The family have become strangers to joy and inevitably the anorexic believes she is responsible, a belief which if not overtly stated is equally not denied."[9] Nevertheless, parents must fight against despair and remind themselves constantly that any tiny bit of weight gain, any modest improvement in behavior, is in fact a triumph. "Each one [weight gain or improvement in behavior] is the result of autonomous action, of a decision freely made by the anorexic herself and worth a pound of flesh produced by tube feeding because there is no secret resolve to shed it again as soon as possible. Nothing has been done *to* the anorexic. She is, slowly and painfully, working her own way out of the anorexic trap."[10]

THREE

THE SPECIAL PROBLEMS OF THE BINGE EATER

Both therapists and researchers on eating disorders agree that it is harder for families to help the binge eater than the self-starver. Nevertheless, there are things that parents, husbands, and others close to the binge eater can do. In order to help, it is first important to know what the binge eater feels, why she does what she does, and what the family can and cannot do to help. Self-starvers do not all continue to lose weight relentlessly to the point of collapse or death. There can come a time when a sufferer breaks her own rules and starts to cram into her mouth some forbidden sweet stuff or other fattening food. The moment when control snaps may come very late for some sufferers and very early for others.[1]

There is a commonly held view that some binge eaters were formerly starvers. However, many are "pure" binge/purgers; that is, their eating disorder began with binge eating rather than starving. Certainly the popular literature frequently points out that many young women start binge eating and purging when they learn about it from friends—or from the popular literature. Many psychologists disagree. Their view is that the binge eater who appears never to have been a starver is actually one who tried to starve but could not, or someone who had been "merely" trying to diet but not succeeding, until she found this highly efficient way of having her cake and getting rid of it too. One fact that supports this theory is that the number of binge eaters appears to be increasing much more rapidly than that of self-starvers. Recent estimates suggest that 5 to 10 percent of college women alone in the United States are regularly gorging and vomiting. This may be due partly to "contagion" or "copycatting," but is more likely due to the number of starvers who have moved on to binge eating.

Agreement is not general on whether starvers and bingers differ in their personalities or on whether they differ in the reasons for their predisposition to an eating disorder. It is also not clear why some people binge and purge almost from the very beginning while some never do.

For some experts, starving and binging/purging is part of a spectrum of eating disorders that share certain fundamental features. According to Dr. Arnold Anderson of Johns Hopkins University, whether an individual is a food restricter or a food binger is mainly related to "the underlying personality features of the patient and the chronicity of the illness."[2] Both are related to excessive social pressures toward overvaluing slimness. Other common features are the fear of fatness, preoccupation with weight and calories, and the use of food and weight control to deal with developmental crises and emotional distress.

The beliefs and values of people who binge and purge resemble those of people who starve. They evaluate their self-worth in terms of their weight and shape, and both fear weight gain and fatness. Starvers, however, strongly prefer extreme thinness, whereas binge eaters are often satisfied with slightly below average weight or even normal weight—so long as it does not go above normal. Abnormal beliefs about body shape are common to both.

Nevertheless, there are important differences between the two kinds of eating disorders. To start, the starver's problem is visible: it is not difficult to tell the difference between a girl who is just thin and one who is abnormally thin because of an eating disorder. (The rare exception is one who is abnormally thin due to serious illness.) The binge eater, on the other hand, may go totally unrecognized. She may look normal or just a trifle underweight, and even those closest to her may not know (at least not for some time) what is going on. The starver flaunts her condition; the purger has "a dirty little secret."

Dr. Anderson notes other differences between the two kinds of eating disorders:

> More and more studies are showing that there are consistent differences in personality and sensory awareness between the two. It is easier to be a food restricter either if hunger and other sensations are perceived less strongly or if there is greater ability to control natural responses. The inability to perceive inner feeling states (hunger, anxiety, sadness or anger) and the greater ability to exercise will to control urges to eat characterizes the food restricting anorectic patient. In contrast, greater awareness of inner states and/or lessened ability to control urges and impulses characterizes the bulimic personality, independent of other features.[3]

Dr. Anderson also points out that binge eaters are usually somewhat older at the time they begin their binging than are those at the time they begin starving, and that there is often a family history of depression and weight or eating problems.[4]

Another study has tabulated the frequency of emotionally unhealthy symptoms in the binge eater as follows: Pathological guilt, 94 percent; worrying, 94; poor concentration, 80; obsessional ideas and rumination, 80; nervous tension, 80; tiredness, 77; self-deprecation, 74; irritability, 74; lack of self-confidence with people, 65; depressed mood, 62; social with-drawal, 62; hopelessness, 60; inefficient thinking, 60; restless-ness and fidgeting, 54.[5]

What seems apparent to the long-time observer of eating disorders is that once binge eating and purging is established, certain other behavior patterns also differ sharply from those of starvers. One important difference arises from the fact that starvation and binge/purging carry different "moral" connota-tions, both for the people who do them and for those around them. Self-starvation, for instance, echoes the ascetic religious commitment of saints and martyrs or the humane convictions of people like Gandhi and, more recently, Soviet dissidents and other political protesters. Binge eating and purging are seen by the binger as self-indulgent and disgusting. The starver can be proud of her willpower and capacity for control over physical impulses, and may be admired by those who wish they could do the same. The binge/purger feels she has reason only to be ashamed. The starver's condition is highly visible; she could not conceal her self-starvation if she wanted to. The binge eater usually has a normal appearance—she can hide her unpleasant secret more easily. People can see that a self-starver is having three peas and a lettuce leaf for dinner; the binge eater can dine out socially, eat a normal meal, then secretly get rid of it. Later, in the privacy of her home or room, she can supplement her dinner with six bags of potato chips, three bologna sandwiches, a whole chocolate cake, and four boxes of Oreos.

Because of the nature of their illness, binge eaters are far more deceitful than self-starvers. They tend to deny that they are binge eating and purging, long after the evidence is compel-ling and others confront them with it. The financial demands of huge quantities of foods often lead to theft. Parents also complain that binge eaters are unconcerned about neatness and hygiene in the home, that they hide food in their closets, under the bed, behind furniture—and often leave it there until it goes bad. They may eat food that was being saved for someone else or had been planned for the family meal, only to deny later that they ate it. Binge eaters are also more likely than starvers to be addicted to alcohol or drugs.

One of the most bizarre and frightening kinds of abnormal behavior among binge eaters is self-mutilation or self-injury. The overwhelming disgust and guilt the purger sometimes feels after a binge/purge episode may lead her to bang her head against the wall, rub her hands and arms against a rough surface until the skin is raw and bleeding, or stub out cigarettes on her thighs.[6] The physical pain puts an end, for the time being, "to the intolerable mental, spiritual, and emotional distress which they do not know how to bear. . . . The need to cope practically with the self-inflicted injury somehow gets the sufferer out of the abyss of self-hatred which she felt threatened the disintegration of her whole personality."[7]

Other differences between starvers and binge eaters are that the former are less sexually active, deny their hunger, are obsessive and more introverted. Binge eaters are often more sexually active (though frequently without a satisfactory emotional involvement), more aware of hunger, and more impulsive and outgoing. While binge eaters and purgers appear on the average to be more "functional"—that is, to be normally continuing their education or employment—they are also more prone to "blue moods."

There is little knowledge or understanding of what triggers the first binge/purge and starts the terrible pattern of overeating, vomiting, guilt, and more overeating. Sometimes it is an unusual stress, loss of a parent through death or divorce, breaking up with a boyfriend, exhaustion, or perhaps just the body finally rebelling against severe and abnormal deprivation. Whatever the circumstance, what matters is the starver's reaction to it. "Without pausing even for a moment to consider the wisdom of what they are trying to do, the universal response of those anorexics who have binged for the first time is to redouble their efforts to exercise control."[8] If they were allowing themselves an egg for lunch before the binge, then afterwards they will eat only the white and throw away the yolk. "It has not occurred to a single sufferer to stop and wonder whether it might be better to do something different instead. In this attitude lies the seeds of failure. Anything a human being accomplishes by the exercise of willpower alone, against the pull of natural inclinations, will not be sustained for long." Thus the first binge will be followed by a second. "We are now certain that the length and ferocity of the subsequent binges are directly proportional to the severity and duration of the preceding periods of fasting. Patients have eventually developed patterns where they live for a week or more on nothing but black coffee and then empty the parental larder in a twelve hour marathon of non-stop eating. They then return to the black coffee diet feeling guilty and disgusting."[9]

When the first binge is followed by another and then another, the binge eater is confronted with a terrible reality—she is gaining weight. Her terror of fatness and her humiliation and disgust at herself for overeating combine to force her to seek some way of counteracting the results. Sooner or later she finds it in purging—usually by vomiting. At first she has to stick a finger or two down her throat or drink salt water. The more she vomits, however, the easier it becomes. Experienced vomiters have merely to stand over the toilet and tense their stomach muscles to vomit with ease. After a while vomiting becomes a conditioned response, which automatically follows once the stomach has reached a certain stage of fullness. When she reaches this stage, the binge eater may not even be able to keep down a meal she does not want to throw up, or can do so only "with a struggle that brings sweat to the sufferer's forehead."[10]

Regularly repeated vomiting brought on by sticking a finger down the throat can cause callouses on the hand where the top teeth rub or press against the skin. It also destroys the enamel of the teeth by exposure to stomach acid. The sufferer may first notice that her teeth (especially the ones in the front of the upper jaw) have become sensitive to hot or cold foods. Damaged teeth can be crowned, but eventually the crowns will be eroded, too. Before this happens the vomiter should be well warned. She may not know that constant vomiting has this effect on the teeth. In particular, if she is living at home and dependent on her parents, she should be made to understand that money for tooth repair is not unlimited—nor is the number of times teeth can be repaired.

In fact, constant binging and purging can seriously effect several organs that are sensitive to potassium loss and dehydration, including the kidneys and the brain. The esophagus can become severely irritated by acid, and chemical abnormalities can cause seizures. Some people have thought that binge eating was associated with a fundamental seizure disorder such as epilepsy, and many parents have wasted time and money taking their child for neurological examinations because she was having seizures, only to discover no evidence of epilepsy. The seizures are a result of the binge/purging, not the cause.

Some people can't vomit. They turn to laxatives. "There is an inevitable escalation here, too. The bowel becomes tolerant of the initial dose of purgatives and no longer responds. The sufferer doubles the dose and is relieved when once more the technique works and she or he spends most of the next day in the lavatory."[11] But sooner or later the dose will have to be increased again. Some laxative abusers reach the point where they are taking thirty to fifty times the acceptable daily dose.

This has damaging long-term effects. It leads to poisoning of the nerve endings supplying the muscle fibers in the intestine. This results in failure of the conductive network so that the bowel can no longer produce the normal coordinated waves of contraction. Elimination becomes more and more difficult. "One of our more unexpected clinical findings was that patients who have regularly used larger-than-normal quantities of laxatives develop a characteristic distension of their upper digestive tract after eating anything like a normal meal. 'It's suddenly just as though she's got a hollow melon in her tummy,' was one husband's description of his wife's state after a rare evening out."[12]

Along with this bloating comes abdominal discomfort, sometimes so severe that the binge eater can't work or carry on normal activities. This distension, which comes on shortly after eating and is clearly visible to the observer, is absolute proof that the binge eater is abusing laxatives. It is also an absolute signal that help is needed immediately. Fortunately, the damage can be reversed if treated in time and correctly. The laxative abuser should not stop "cold turkey." A gradual reduction in dose allows the bowel to adjust. Stopping suddenly, on the other hand, can make the bowel stop functioning with uncomfortable suddenness that may result in a painful medical crisis.

A telltale sign of vomiting is facial swelling due to enlargement of the salivary glands, which makes the sufferer look as if she has mumps. This is especially striking when it occurs in a vomiter who is severely underweight. The tragedy of this symptom is that someone can be losing weight, steadily increasing her food restriction, vomiting more and more often, and yet find it possible to convince those around her that she is not increasing her abuses because her face is not getting thinner. Knowledge of swelling due to excessive vomiting should prevent families from making this mistake.

The vomiter or laxative abuser can seriously upset her body chemistry. When food is purged, gastric juices and intestinal fluids are also expelled. To offset the loss, the body "borrows" needed chemicals from other parts of the body, and the net result is a serious loss of potassium, a substance absolutely necessary for the normal functioning of nerve fibers and muscle cells. The result is severe muscle weakening. A binge eater may suddenly complain that she cannot walk upstairs or that

she cannot lift an even modest weight. Complaints of unexpected bodily fatigue or of sensations like pins and needles in
the limbs or around the mouth are serious warning signs. If
this stage is reached, it must be corrected quickly by a physician. There is a potential threat to life in this condition. If the
heart muscle is affected, it can simply stop working, and the
result is sudden death.

One of the things that can be startling and baffling to
parents is that during the starving phase, most starvers are
extremely thrifty. They hoard money. They are unwilling to
spend it—or to see others spend it—on anything but absolute
necessities. The sudden reversal of this behavior should be a
clue to parents that the starver has become a binge eater.
Bingers will not only throw away their savings on enormous
quantities of food, but will begin working overtime or babysitting every night. Those old enough to have credit cards may
use them to their limits. When their own resources fail, they
will turn to others, always surreptitiously. They may take
money from mother's pocketbook or father's wallet. They may
steal from employers. Shoplifting of food or of goods that can
be sold for food is common.

The financial mess, the worry about how to pay for the next
binge, the guilt over the irresponsibility or dishonesty of their
behavior—all these lead to further worry, depression, and anxiety, which the sufferer can only relieve through further binges.
"When the binge is over and awareness of the rest of her life
returns the wretchedness of the impact of these thoughts and
feelings cannot be overestimated. This is the moment above all
others when suicide may be attempted."[13]

Like their sister starver, binge eaters will often say, "Mom is
the villain." This has been the overwhelming conclusion whenever eating disorders in children are examined. According to
two well-known therapists, Marlene Boskind-White and William C. White, Jr., "Researchers and clinicians, and even
feminist writers, are likely to hold mothers responsible; all

deplore the controlling mother who is seen as 'perfectionist, domineering, and overinvolved' with her children."[14] Both therapists call this entrenched view "myopic, destructive, and unjust." They find it especially destructive for the binge/ purgers. Putting the blame on mothers may afford a certain satisfaction, but it means the binge eater is focusing her energy on the past. She is concentrating on the whys, the earlier causes of her aberrant behavior patterns, rather than asking herself what she is gaining by continuing them now.[15]

Mother as the root of all evil is only one of the myths embraced by binge eaters and purgers. Among their many misconceptions, the most common are these:

1. "Binge eating and purging is a disease, a mental illness." Women would like to believe this. It means it is being "done" to them and someone else must undo it. Boskind-White and White are convinced that it is a learned behavior, a *habit* that can be exceedingly difficult to give up. Because it is learned, however, it can be unlearned.

2. "It has taken years for me to develop these behavior patterns, therefore, it will take years to stop." This is self-defeating, and if your daughter clings to it, she gives up any chance of finding more productive behaviors. With help she can learn to stress more healthy alternatives. It is helpful to point out that women who have been chronic bingers for fifteen to twenty years have curtailed or eliminated the behavior in a few months.

3. "Unless I understand why I binge and purge, I'll never be able to give it up." Although the search for understanding is fascinating and occasionally rewarding, it typically results in frustration and failure. Obsession with *why* consumes valuable energy and leaves the binge-eater vulnerable to continued failure. It is far more helpful to concentrate on what the binge eater is getting out of her behavior. What are the pay-offs?

4.   "If I'm to give up binging and purging, I must do it on my own." Self-reliance is inappropriate. The binge eater is simply not capable of sustaining herself independently. On the contrary, she is most vulnerable when she is alone. She should be encouraged to seek out those who care for her and will give her their support when she feels a compulsion to binge. Many therapists recommend "contracts" between several binge eaters, in which they arrange to make themselves available to each other in times of crisis.

5.   "As a binge eater, I am powerless in the face of food." This is not only illogical, it prevents her from becoming self-motivated. A binge eater can be shown that former bingers and purgers have, within a few weeks or months, developed the capacity to enjoy a palatable meal without disastrous consequences.

6.   "When I stop binging and purging, everything will be fine." There is no way this expectation can be fulfilled. Furthermore, such a belief holds the *syndrome* accountable rather than the *person* who chooses to engage in the behavior. By maintaining that the insidious uncontrollable disease process makes her life miserable, the binge eater commits herself to despair.[16]

Part of the reason that binge eating and purging become so chronic is that the binge eater is seeking escape from the normal pain of life. The perfectionist and self-hater in her believes that if her life has any pain in it, it is a failure, and this is her fault. When the binge eater accepts the reality that no life is without discomfort, even pain, and that even if she does not binge/purge she will sometimes feel pain, she will have to accept that she is not perfect. She will also have to accept the fact that sometimes she herself will be the inadvertent cause of some of that pain.

This is one of several reasons why therapy for binge/purging can be difficult. To begin with, the binge eater does not want to give up the "illness" as the scapegoat for all of her troubles, nor does she want to admit that she is imperfect. Many also falter or regress after they are in therapy because they discover that even after they stop binge eating, their troubles don't all go away. Experienced therapists point out to the binge eater that at the beginning of therapy, she may feel worse because she won't yet have an alternative stress-relieving behavior to replace the one she is giving up. But most agree that it is necessary to *stop the behavior* before therapy can begin to be effective.

Parents who are trying to get their self-starving or binge eating child into therapy need to know what the therapeutic goals are. This way they can encourage their child in the right direction, cooperate with the therapist, and avoid conflicting with the gains made in each session. If they are helping the child find a therapist, they also need to know what kind of therapy is currently available.

Much of the material in our seventh chapter is relevant to therapy for both starvation and binging. There are, however, some approaches used for binge eating only that need to be described. Most experts agree that binge eating and purging share common elements with addictions such as smoking and alcoholism. Many binge eaters also suffer acutely from anxiety, depression, social phobias, impulsivity, mood swings, sensitivity to rejection, and problems in their relationships with family and other intimates. Therapy must take these complications into account and deal with each binge eater as an individual. Not all people will respond to the same therapy in the same way. "Experience has shown that many patients are not well served by either a narrow therapeutic focus or by assembly line treatment programs."[17]

Most therapy has two basic goals. The eating behavior is closely linked to the underlying psychological problem. The behavior is caused by the problem and, in turn, aggravates it. Thus both the patient's behavior and feelings need to change.

Behavior that is self-defeating and demoralizing must be reduced or eliminated, but changing the behavior is not enough—the self-hatred and self-contempt must also be dealt with.

Among the techniques a therapist may introduce to help the binge eater deal with her behavior are several that can be encouraged and supported by the family.

One is delay. If she can be taught to "wait out" the urge to binge, this urge will

> follow a natural cycle of increasing, like a wave, and then coming back down. It feels intolerable on the way up, but it eventually decreases. Sometimes the urge can be waited out with a therapist or trusted friend, but eventually the patient must do it alone. Patients must learn that they do not have to respond immediately to the urge—it will *not* keep increasing—it *will* come down—they can tolerate the discomfort. The goal should be clear; there is no promise that patients will be free of urges to binge, but there is realistic hope that they will be able to deal with them constructively. A false promise that urges to binge will completely disappear leads to disappointment and disillusionment. Learning to wait out an urge also gives the ego more strength and confidence. Some patients are amazed that they can wait out the experience. The goal is not to fear the urge but to understand it, choose a different response to it, and ultimately to prevent it if possible by changing some of the contributing factors.[18]

Other techniques include education designed to help the binge eater change her maladaptive attitudes about food. She may be instructed to introduce new foods into her diet to break habitual patterns. Techniques to help her learn self-control may include keeping a diary, self-monitoring eating behavior, positive reinforcement with praise, and relaxation training to help her control impulsive behavior.

There is some question about the overall effectiveness of these largely behavioral approaches which rely on changes of habit rather than changes of feeling based on insight into the underlying emotional problems of the binge eater. There are no carefully controlled scientific studies of the outcome of this—or any other—kind of therapy. Some behavioral therapists report a high proportion of success, but it must be remembered that the patients in such studies may have been very motivated to change and that these therapists were probably both highly experienced and highly involved with their patients. In choosing a therapist it is important to know that "not all behavior therapy is as elegantly or competently applied as by those who contribute to the literature, and unsuccessful treatment cases or series are rarely published."[19]

After years of experience, many therapists have concluded that individual therapy may not work as well for binge eaters as it does for starvers. Some have experimented successfully with group therapy following the pattern developed by Marlene Boskind-White and William C. White, Jr. Members of their groups support and learn from each other, but their treatment program is still individualized for each patient. The general emphasis is on "payoffs"—of which there are very few. The binge eater can learn to recognize that, in fact, she gets nothing useful or healthy out of her behavior. Gorging and purging mostly come to be seen either as avoidance behaviors or as means of punishing oneself or others.

When several group members have identified what maintains their binging, they usually begin to identify with each other. Their sense of sisterhood and comraderie is thus enhanced. It is not absolutely necessary for each woman to discover what she is deriving from her destructive behavior. Some are not ready to acknowledge this, some feel incapable of doing so, and others already know but have done nothing to effect change. Those who do know, often begin to consider alternatives to binging. Those who do not know can observe those who do. Later, they too may be able to address this particular issue.

The therapists also point out that there are few behaviors

that are irreversible. If the old ways are not working, why not give some new ones a try? If the patients do not like the new ones, they can always try others, or go back to the old. The new and unfamiliar are certainly uncomfortable for everybody. This is especially true for binge eaters.[20]

Binge eaters are less often treated in the hospital than are starvers. They are not usually in medical danger because of extreme low weight. And like people with other "impulse" disorders (such as alcoholism and drug abuse), they do not adjust well to hospitalization and seem to do better in outpatient therapy. However, a binge eater may need a brief period in the hospital if she has extreme metabolic abnormalities, serious potassium deficiency, is markedly depressed, or expresses an intention to harm herself. As far as therapy for the eating behavior is concerned, there seems little to be gained from inpatient management along the lines used for self-starvation. Any benefits gained tend to be short-lived. If a binge eater needs to be hospitalized for any of the reasons just given, hospitalization should be brief and regarded as preparation for a formal outpatient treatment program.[21]

Many binge eaters with bulimia are given appetite suppressants or antidepressants. While there can be no doubt that these people have an excessive desire for food, very few of them report that appetite suppressants are helpful. One reason for caution is that some binge eaters have a definite propensity toward alcohol- and drug-dependence. Since many binge eaters suffer from depression, it might appear reasonable to prescribe antidepressants. However, mood seems to be directly related to the degree of control over eating, and in most cases the depression lifts in response to psychotherapy. Antidepressants might be used if severe depression persists, but there's a problem here as to which drug to prescribe. Most antidepressants tend to increase carbohydrate craving and weight gain, both of which are poorly tolerated by binge eaters. Other psychopharmaceuticals often prescribed for this condition are dangerous because of the severe reactions caused by eating certain foods in combination with the drug. Binge eaters usually cannot be trusted to follow these restrictions. They tend, in fact, to binge on exactly those foods that are prohibited.

What can parents, husbands, friends, and lovers do to help?

Many therapists believe that there is very little family and friends can do for the binge eater in a direct way.

> Advice, recommendations, and threats only cause the woman to become more defiant of or dependent on those who are trying to help. Well-intentioned loved ones often set themselves up for a great deal of pain and frustration when they assume the role of caretaker. Do not take responsibility for her behavior by trying to fix her! If you fail, you and she both feel you are incompetent. If you succeed, the "victim" is dependent upon you. It is a no-win situation that is exceedingly hard to resist, particularly for well-integrated, successful, caring people. The bulimarexic must initiate the process of change by herself making a commitment to doing something on her own behalf.[22]

Parents or other intimates can help in small, sometimes indirect ways. Most of the suggestions in chapter 4 are applicable to both self-starvers and binge eaters. In addition, there are specific suggestions for the latter.

The first, most important thing is to bring the secret out into the open. If you are aware that your child is binge eating and purging, then you can be sure *she* knows *you* know. To continue to act as if you are blind about it is to suggest to her that you are stupid, or that you do not care and do not want to help. It also suggests to her that you do not disapprove of her deceit. Once the problem has been confronted and brought out into the open, anything you can do to encourage further communication and discussion is worthwhile. Although you cannot threaten, plead, or bully her into getting help, you can make it clear that help is available. You can show her that you will cooperate in working with her condition and that she *can* live a healthier, happier life.

Cooperate by keeping minimal food supplies in the house. Help make it easier for the binge eater to stay out of the kitchen: if it has always been the family gathering place, change your custom—use another room. Most of all, *be there* if she needs to confide in someone. Pay her the compliment of confiding in her as well. Provide support when she is trying to deal with the urge to overeat—keep her busy, stay with her, help her to "ride out the wave." Applaud her successes.

COPING DAY BY DAY

No two families are alike, and no set of rules or advice will be appropriate or relevant to every family. From the experience of a great variety and number of families, starvers, and therapists, however, certain general principles or guidelines emerge. These can be adopted or adapted to a particular family's situation. Among these are the following:

First, Second, and Third: Listen to Her.

The well-known author and lecturer Eric Hoffer was an uneducated longshoreman, whose writings, begun after many years as a manual laborer, astonished observers with their literary style and erudition. Hoffer was once asked if he could explain how this came about. His answer was that as a child he lived with an aunt who was always saying things to him like, "What was that you were telling me yesterday about so-and-so?" or "What do you think of this?" Hoffer comments: "I grew up thinking I had something to say that was worth listening to."

Few starvers grow up with the same advantage. Many starvers were children who received little attention or whose parents or family listened with only half an ear, murmuring some assent now and then, but not really *attending* to what the child was saying. Others suffered the opposite kind of deprivation: too much attention was lavished on them. Overwhelmed with advice, warnings, and unsolicited help, the child was deprived of the opportunity to learn for herself, to develop independence, self-sufficiency, and internal discipline. It is the kind of attention that will make any child eventually burst out with, "Please mother, let me do it myself." This kind of attention does not attend to the child but is always directed outward *at* the child, almost as if the child had no mind, feelings, or solutions of her own.

Such patterns as these do not necessarily lead to eating disorders, though they may certainly contribute. Once an eating disorder has developed, however, it is essential that parents begin learning how to listen to their child's true feelings and thoughts. This does not mean that parents should blindly give in to her demands or expectations, but rather that parents must learn to hear and understand what prompts these demands and what they mean to the child. One of the things the "listening" parent will learn is that the self-starver's misbehavior and tyrannical ways actually fill her with guilt and make her feel like a "bad person." She wants to be helped to stop them.

It may become very difficult to listen with sincere attention and concern when the starver comes to you for the millionth time with the same complaint, the same plaintive appeal for help, or the same accusation that, "You made me this way!" Your urge sometimes will be to say, "Not now, I'm busy," or even, "Not again!" This urge must be resisted. This does not mean that whenever she wants to be listened to, you must drop whatever you are doing, however inconvenient that may be, and devote your full attention to her for however long she wants to claim it. It does mean that you must handle the situation with impeccable sensitivity and care. You *must* convey the impression that you are very much concerned with what she has to say. But you may then tell her that at the moment you cannot give your attention (because your mind is too divided by other concerns or worries, because dinner is about to burn, because you have to pick somebody up at the station). Tell her you want to talk with her when you can really take the time and energy to listen. If you manage to convince her that you are not just pushing her aside, she will probably agree to a postponement. You must be sure to honor your promise to talk with her at the earliest possible moment.

Listening does not mean listening only when the discussion is about her problem, and it does not mean listening with half an ear. The self-starver is easily and deeply hurt by attention that is half-given even in a casual conversation, by replies that are just "uh huh" rather than a thoughtful, appropriate contribution that demonstrates your true interest in what she is saying. You must give her genuine attention, but *must not feign interest.* If you are really bored by the topic, you might try gently and naturally easing the conversation into another path; or simply say, "I don't know much about this and can't discuss it very intelligently."

Listening also means trying to hear what she *means,* not just what she is saying. It means being alert to hidden messages. One mother reported a scene that occurred repeatedly with her daughter, whom she was trying to persuade to enter therapy. Every time the mother urged her to see a therapist, the child became angry, shouting, "You're trying to tell me that if I don't get therapy, I'll never get better. I might as well give up hope." The mother, frightened by the violence of the reaction and by what might happen if the child did "give up hope," always backed down immediately. She would say, "No, I'm not telling you that's the only way, just the quickest way." This response only seemed to make the child angrier. After many months, and after the mother herself consulted a therapist for advice, she realized that the child had *wanted* her to make therapy an ultimatum. In that way, the part of her that resisted would have no choice, and the other part of her—that really wanted help—would have parental approval for seeking it outside the family.

Listening may also mean paying attention to nonverbal messages and clues from behavior. One mother described how her daughter had persistently denied that she was a binge eater. After many weeks, the mother began noticing that the daughter kept leaving the container of household cleanser and the toilet brush out in the open, rather than in the closet where they had always been kept. "I know she's vomiting and then cleaning up," the mother told a parents' group, "but I don't understand why she leaves the cleaning things out." Other parents, more experienced, immediately pointed out to her that her daughter was probably trying to send a message: "I can't actually admit that I'm vomiting, but I'm trying to get you to notice. I can't ask for help, but I need it." Another mother told of an even more dramatic example of "signaling." Her daughter vomited in the family bathroom and did not clean up at all.

Listening, finally, means that members of the family should learn to listen to each other as well as to the starver. There is a tendency in some families (and not just those with a starver) to be what psychologists call "enmeshed." They are extremely close; they practically live inside each other's clothes. In such families there are often unfortunate habit patterns: one family member tells another what the second feels and thinks; the family members finish each other's sentences, they interrupt, they do not listen to a whole sentence but begin answering it before it's finished—even though the ending might not have been what they thought it was. Such families can be said not to communicate at all, because all they are listening to is themselves, not each other. Such behavior further heightens a starver's sense of isolation and her feeling that nobody cares about her feelings or her thoughts. Such patterns, for that matter, are not particularly healthy for anybody else in the family.

What listening really adds up to is that you let the starver know that you care about what she has to say, that her ideas, opinions, and feelings are valued because she is valued.

Be Honest.

"I never know if I'm saying the right thing," a parent says. "One day I say something and it's all right. The next day I say the same thing and everything explodes." Parents become acutely aware of a starving child's sensitivities and "trigger points," things that are likely to set off a tantrum or a barrage of angry accusations. Confrontations become so frequent and so painful that avoidance becomes the intuitive response. "I feel as if I'm always walking across a minefield," parents commonly say. "I tiptoe all the time." Unfortunately, the harder you try to say and do "the right thing," the worse off you are. You will get no gratitude, because the starver (in common with other children and adolescents but even more so) can spot phoniness in the pitch dark. If you say you don't mind making another trip to the store for something she needs, she can tell immediately if you really do find it inconvenient and are resentful of her demands. Her response will be anger, guilt, and contempt. Which is her real parent and which is the phony? Which of your statements is genuine and honest and which one is faked for the occasion? And most important: what is the message the child gets if you can smother some minor feeling and pretend to feel different in order to avoid conflict? "No, I don't really mind if you borrowed my best silk scarf and got spots on it." The message is clear to the child and it is terrifying: "This person is not honest and can't be trusted. Therefore when she says I look pretty, she thinks I'm ugly. When she says she loves me, she really hates me. After all, who could love an unloveable person like me, who just borrowed her best scarf and got spots on it?"

Conscious attempts to say the thing you think will please her are harmful for another reason. Spontaneity and risk-taking are among the things starvers find impossible; they find them threatening and dangerous. Thus it is vital for the starver to learn again how to be spontaneous, to do something just for the fun of it, to perform an act that might not work out exactly as expected. When parents bottle up their own spontaneity, they send a loud message to the child: "You're right. Spontaneity is bad. Expressing feelings honestly is bad—you could get hurt that way. Avoid them the way we do."

Honesty must extend to all members of the family. Even if you are totally honest (within the boundaries of kindness and respect) with your child, she will think you are lying if she sees you behaving or speaking insincerely to others.

Parents Must Be United.

This does not mean ganging up on your child. In fact, it is often best for one parent to handle a particular scene and for the other parent to back out or refrain from interfering. Three-way confrontations are fraught with peril. Either she will feel outnumbered and become even more terrified, or she will grasp the opportunity for "triangulation," which entails one person playing the other two against each other. But it must be clear that the absent or refraining parent respects the involved parent's statements, rules, and attitudes. Parents must be exceptionally alert to any sign of a difference of opinion regarding the handling of their child. They must discuss it and work it out honestly and *in private,* never in front of the child, and especially never in anger. It will not only frighten her (because starvers are often acutely uneasy about the possibility of a family break-up), it will add to her guilt to see that she has caused you to quarrel.

One of the many dangers of having a self-starving child is that the parents' concern over her and their sense of frustration and helplessness may begin to overwhelm their self-confidence and common sense. This in turn may lead them to question their own and each other's values and opinions. A lot of healthy self-examination is helpful, but too much neurotic self-doubt will make a parent much less capable of dealing with a starver's behavior. Furthermore, this self-doubt will eventually communicate itself to the child.

One parent may unwittingly start blaming the other parent for the child's difficulties. This can only erode your relationship and signal to the child—regardless of who is being blamed—that *somebody* has to be blamed. She will undoubtedly decide that it is really she who is being blamed. Starvers can't help feeling that they are "bad" people who are the cause of everything wrong.

Honest differences of opinion, discussed reasonably and with affection, can be worked out or accommodated. Minor differences can be allowed to stand. After all, nobody agrees completely with anyone else about everything. Trying to agree completely will only cause frustration and once again indicate to the child that you are not being honest. On the other hand, parents who have significant and longstanding differences in values, especially about child-rearing, may find it extremely difficult to cope with their self-starving child. These parents should definitely seek professional help. This is particularly true if these significant differences had not been revealed previously and have only emerged as a result of the child's self-starvation. She will interpret this as another sign of her badness and guilt. She will not recognize it as something that was always there but will assume it was something she caused.

Keep Promises.

Self-starvers cannot trust themselves. They cannot trust their ability to control their lives and their impulses. They "know" if they eat one cracker they will eat the whole box. Therefore they need to find trust elsewhere until they learn self-trust. They must be reassured of your trustworthiness by repeated, consistent keeping of promises and commitments. One good way to make sure you never break a promise is never to make one you cannot be sure to keep; and always point out the conditions under which it might not be possible to keep your promise. Say, "I think I can manage that, and I'll try my hardest, but if I have to work late or if my train is delayed, I might not make it." Of all the promises one must avoid making, the most significant are those that have to do with her condition and her recovery. While parents must *always* express confidence in recovery, they must never make specific predictions (which to her are promises). They must not say, "Yes, of course you'll be all right in time to go to college in the fall." You have no way of knowing whether she will be well enough to go to school in the fall. If she is not, after you have assured her she would be, she will feel you have betrayed her. "All you have to do is see a therapist, and you'll be fine." This latter remark is particularly dangerous. It implies that the therapist is going to "fix it." This means first of all that your daughter is going to be once again under somebody else's control. Second, it means that she neither has the capability of nor the responsibility for doing any of the "fixing" herself. Indeed, therapy for self-starving entails an enormous amount of hard work on the starver's part. Nothing you say should suggest to her that she doesn't have to do anything herself.

Do Not Argue with Her Too Much.

Self-starvers desperately need to find validation for their feelings. They are so confused about what they feel and why, and have so little confidence in their own ideas or opinions, that any contradiction is unsettling, even frightening. This is not to suggest that a parent agree uncritically with anything a child says. You certainly can have different opinions, but you shouldn't disagree with her opinion of how she feels or tell her she shouldn't feel that way. The father whose daughter objected to his rattling the pages of his newspaper while she was studying told a parents' meeting that they often had violent battles over this. He would become extremely angry when she asked him not to do it, telling her that she was being outrageously oversensitive and that this little noise couldn't possibly bother anyone. These confrontations generally ended with the starver going to her room to cry in total defeat. In fact, every member of the family found the noise irritating, but had been unwilling to speak up because they were intidimated by the father's anger. Even if they had not felt this way, the father should have taken into account people's different sensitivities. Some things that might not bother him could bother others, and vice versa. It is crucial for parents and other family members to confirm each other's right to feel certain ways. One way to handle conflicts that arise because of differences is to strike a deal that recognizes the starver's needs but helps remind her that everyone has feelings and needs. The father, for example, could agree not to rattle his newspaper and, in turn, she could agree to refrain from doing something that annoys him.

In some families, the tendency to deny the validity of other people's feelings can become severe, and for the starver, overwhelming. For example, one girl described how her parents bought her a carpet as a gift. It was a secondhand carpet and apparently cleaned with some chemical that smelled bad in rainy weather. The girl said to her parents, "You know, this carpet really smells." And her mother replied, "No, it doesn't."

"Well damn, if every time that carpet stank, I didn't smack myself and say, 'It doesn't smell.' That just sums it up—sums up the fact that the reality was my mother's," the girl later told her therapist. "I was so busy existing for feedback, any kind of feedback. Tell me I'm right, tell me I'm wrong, just tell me! I need someone to tell me because I don't exist if you don't tell me. . . . The carpet that *stank, it did stink,* because it smelled to me and I *know* the carpet smells."[1]

Avoid Actions and Words that Foster the Starver's
Tendency to Be Self-centered.

Nobody else in the family would be allowed to lock others out of the bathroom for hours or to usurp the television set every evening. The starver must be expected to observe family rules even when they are inconvenient to her, just as others observe rules when inconvenient. This is by no means a denial of her feelings and needs; it is a recognition that she is not the center of the universe but a part of it like everyone. You must not ignore her needs or give them lower priority than the needs of others, but they must not be allowed to negate the rights of others. It is helpful (in all families, not just the families of starvers), to make clear what the family standards are rather than allowing members to guess from observation or experience. It is important to establish expectations for behavior in noncritical ways. One doesn't say to a child, "Stop playing with your food, it's disgusting." One says "In this family, people don't play with their food."

Encourage the Starver in Every Possible Way
to Uncover Her Own Resources.

Help her to see and accept her own capacity to feel and to make judgments and decisions. Many starvers do things because they think they are expected to, not because they want to or because they see the utility of doing them. Hilde Bruch tells of a young girl who entered her office, "her face shining as if something great and exciting had happened." The girl then announced that after school that day, she had taken a shower because *she* wanted to. It was a new and different feeling for her. Many children, not just starvers, are accustomed to doing as they are told. "Wear your galoshes. Drink your milk. Wash your face." Parents of starvers should approach these "required behavior" situations from a different point of view (as should most parents). Instead of insisting that the child do something "because we say so," it's better to point out how it will benefit her. The classic childhood example of this is that you do not tell a child to wear galoshes because she must, but because if she does not wear them her feet will get cold and wet.

It is particularly important that the self-starver carry some responsibility in the family. It helps make her feel a more secure part of the family, it also tells her you believe she is capable of carrying responsibility, and it counterbalances the family's tendency to treat the starver as "different."

Try to Maintain Normalcy.

At the first sign that the starver is making unreasonable demands on the rest of the family or subverting family customs to her own needs, parents should set reasonable but firm limits. Yes, you will buy her special brand of low-calorie ice cream when you go to the grocery. No, you will not go out for it at midnight. You'll be glad to get any special foods she wants—if she lets you know in time, or if she writes it on the family grocery list in the kitchen. The starver must be treated with love and respect and her emotional needs must be met, but not by treating her as "different" from other family members, not if it means somebody else's needs must be sacrificed. Yes, you will try to keep the TV set tuned down to a reasonable level. No, she may not have private use of the family room on the night her sister has already invited friends for a party. It is disastrous for the starver as well as the family if your social life gives way to her exaggerated demands. Parents should be particularly careful not to stop engaging in their usual outside social activities—going to the theatre, having dinner out once a week, going away for the weekend now and then. The starver needs to see that grown-ups have a life of their own, that they have fun, that there is something attractive about being an adult—and that no child has the power to dictate or severely alter established habits and activities. Having too much power is frightening for a child, even more so to a self-starver.

People who have had no experience with the skill starvers develop in taking over the family reins may be surprised to be told that they need to maintain their normal social life. They may wonder why they would not just naturally do so. But parents who have been through the experience can tell you that it happens even without your realizing it. First you cancel a weekly dinner out because your child is unusually depressed and needs you to cheer her up or at least keep her from being lonely. A couple of weeks later it happens again; then two weeks in a row, and suddenly, it has been over a month since you went out for dinner. Then you give away your theatre tickets at the last minute because she has been hinting at suicide all day.

Parents must not let themselves fall into this trap—for their own sake as well as their child's. A combination of common sense and ingenuity usually provide the means to avoid it. One couple described how they had made plans months ahead to go to a particularly exciting opening night at the opera, and on the day they were to go, their teen-age daughter wanted them to stay home with her. When they told her they would not cancel their plans, she said, "All right, when you come home I'll be dead." For a moment they almost capitulated, but after a brief private discussion, they told the child that they had no intention of missing this important event that they had been looking forward to so long. But because they loved her and cared very much about her life, they were going to get a babysitter for the evening.

Do Not Reward Her for Her Illness.

This is a major component of maintaining normalcy. One reason the self-starving syndrome can become so solidly established in such a short time is that initially it works. It provides some immediate rewards of considerable importance to the starver. Chief among these is that it sets her apart as "different" and "interesting" to her friends and it attracts the attention and deep concern of her family. Suddenly the child who has felt like "a nothing" is the focus of the family's deepest interest. Furthermore, parents' fears for her health, sanity, and life weaken their usual control over family behavior and allow her to grasp the reins. While having too much power is frightening for a child, taking charge over the family nevertheless gives her at least a brief lift, a feeling of being able to control *something*.

If the family continues to pay her extra attention, to treat her as special and to exempt her from the usual rules of family conduct—if they thus allow her to determine the tone and structure of family life—she will be confirmed in her notion that self-starvation is a rewarding solution to her problem. Conversely, if her behavior is not rewarded by attention and power, if she is suffering constant hunger and getting nothing in return for it, she will be more likely to consider that it is not such a good solution after all.

One mother told my parents' support group a dramatic example of this.

My daughter would starve herself until her stomach was so shrunken it couldn't hold a mustard seed, and then she would go to the donut shop and stuff herself with dozens of donuts. The first time she did this, her stomach blocked, and we had to call an ambulance to take her to the hospital to be pumped out before her stomach burst. She almost died. So did her father and I; we were terrified. When she got out we were so grateful she was still alive we couldn't do enough nice things for her or give her enough love and attention.

This happened three times. The third time, when she came home from the hospital, I told her that the week in the hospital cost $1500 and her father and I had paid that much three times, but we weren't going to pay it again. She had exactly

$1500 in the bank which she had saved from her job. I said she could avoid going to the hospital by not starving and stuffing, but if she ever did have to go again, I would take that money out of the bank, which I was legally entitled to do, and she would pay, not us. If it came to it, I could also take money out of her grandmother's legacy to her. She never went to the hospital again.

Another mother told the same support group about a different response. When her daughter was so thin she couldn't regulate her body temperature, she kept turning the thermostat up. "When I came home from work the house would be like an oven. Our heating bill the first month she did that was three times the normal amount for a winter month. But what could I do? Let her freeze to death? Of course I let her keep turning the heat up. She'd be wrapped in four layers of clothes and shivering with the temperature at 80 degrees, and the rest of us were sweating in short sleeve shirts."

This reaction is understandable enough, but it clearly signals to the child that being "ill" gives her special privileges and allows her to escape the rules and responsibilities that govern "normal" members of the family. As even the most amateur psychologist knows, things that produce unpleasant results are likely to be avoided while those that produce pleasant ones will be repeated. This is not to suggest that parents deliberately try to make life unpleasant for the starver. It simply means that they must not go to extra lengths to protect the starver from the unpleasant consequences of her behavior.

Do Not Punish Her for Her Illness.

The starver does not want to be a tyrant. She is driven. She knows she is making you miserable and she hates herself for it. Do not add to her guilt with remarks such as, "You're ruining your father. He's so miserable he can't work." Or, "You're making me ill, keeping me awake so late every night." Keep your focus on her problem, not on her behavior or her character.

Keep Your Perspective; Set Priorities.

Parents of children with eating disorders may find themselves in what feels like a state of siege. They are trying to handle their jobs, their household duties, their own personal lives and worries, and often the tremendous financial burden imposed by their daughter's therapy. When the minute-by-minute irritations of their daughter's strange and often disruptive behavior are added to this, it is not surprising that parents often lose a sense of balance and proportion.

It is essential to take stock regularly, to ask yourself, "Is this the thing that most demands my attention and energy at the moment?" The parents of a child who had progressed from self-starving to binge/purging finally attended a parents' support group meeting in hopes of finding out how to get professional help. They described their daughter as showing many signs of being ready to accept professional help, and were given a great deal of advice on how to go about getting it. Then the mother described her unhappiness about her daughter's habit of hoarding food in her room: "bags of donuts, potato chips, sometimes a plate of second helpings from dinner." These were tucked under her bed, hidden in her closet, even in her desk drawers.

"I can't stand that mess," the mother said, "and I'm upset about mice or rats or bugs getting into the house. I've nagged and nagged to get her to clean up, but she won't do it."

Members of the parents group advised her that no child should be allowed to do this in her parents' home, and she should be told that she had two choices: to keep food out of her room or to earn money and pay for regular visits from an exterminator. But the group also recommended that in this case, this response would be more appropriate *at some other time.* These parents' most important priority at that moment was finding appropriate professional help for their daughter and taking immediate advantage of her apparent willingness to accept such help. It was not the moment for a confrontation over the daughter's need to hoard food and the parents' need to have some control over hygiene in their home. The daughter might feel threatened and become antagonistic towards her parents. She might take revenge by refusing to go to a therapist after all. The issue at that moment was getting help, not getting the daughter's room tidy. That confrontation could come later, or once the daughter began to progress in therapy, might never need take place.

Do Not Exchange Roles with Her.

Parents may become emotionally depleted by their child's illness and disruptive behavior. As a result, they may send the following message to the child: "We don't have any more strength." According to Steven Levenkron, the child reacts to this by becoming the parent, by giving the parents her emotional support. They, in turn, may welcome this and come to depend on it by giving her too many decisions to make, too many options, and too little support. She begins to see herself as valued for making her own needs subservient to theirs. She feels insecure without the safety of her parents' support, and looks for safety elsewhere—often in rituals of compulsive organizing. In such a situation, parents may need professional help in reevaluating and realigning their relationship with their child. Levenkron especially cautions parents to provide the child with positive messages of strength, calmness, and confidence in their ability to help her. They are to avoid messages that are concealed cries for her help, such as "If you'd only cheer up instead of ruining our day, it will be better for us all."[2]

Admit Mistakes, Confess Faults, Apologize for Hurtful Words or Acts.

It is terribly important for parents to say, "I goofed, I was wrong." Self-starvers seek perfection for themselves. They believe it is possible to achieve perfection. Parents who either believe they are perfect or consistently deny their imperfections only confirm the child's belief in the possibility of perfection, and of the undesirability of having faults. There are many ways of denying one's flaws other than through overt statements such as, "You're wrong, I'm right," or "I couldn't possibly have made a mistake." One common way is by shifting responsibility to someone else. For example, a wife asks her husband several times not to tilt his chair on its back legs at the dinner table because a stand with a valuable vase is directly behind him. After ignoring several requests to stop, he finally leans back too far and knocks over the vase. On being upbraided about this, he retorts, "Well, that was a stupid place to put that vase."

It is crucial for parents to communicate to the child the idea that making a mistake is neither "wrong" nor "bad" but only human. What she also needs to learn is that certain acts have certain consequences and therefore should be avoided. She must be helped to understand that people have to be responsible for their acts. If she throws a plate on the floor and breaks it during a temper tantrum, she must first clean it up and then pay for it out of her allowance or earnings. Having taken responsibility and done whatever possible to undo the damage, her behavior should not only be forgiven but forgotten.

Parents must avoid being moralistic or judgmental about any misbehavior or moodiness, but especially in regard to any of the child's eating quirks. This can be difficult and it may become impossible in the case of the binge eater who can eat—and waste—hundreds of dollars' worth of food in addition to what the family usually buys; or in the case of the starver who throws away food or—quite commonly—feeds it to the family dog under the dinner table. As one mother said, "the thinner she got, the fatter the dog got."

Fathers are perhaps more inclined than mothers to be "explosively irritated when they discover that the carefully thought-out contents of their daughter's lunchbox have been thrown away untasted before she reaches school week after week," say Jill Wellbourn and Joan Purgold of the University of Bristol. "The waste of their money and the fact that their wife's expenditure of time and effort has been rendered useless can make these fathers very angry. They are morally outraged at their daughter's descent into deviousness and dishonesty." But these experts warn that such reactions must be avoided or at least moderated. Moralistic attitudes can only "stiffen the daughter's determination to go on limiting her intake of food. If anything does change as a result of father's outburst, it will be in the direction of stricter limits and the imposition of more rigid controls. After all, why should anyone change their beliefs and behavior to please someone who shouts and scolds?"[3]

Do Not Allow Schooling to Be Disrupted.

Dropping out of school is common among self-starvers. Sometimes they are physically unable to continue school work either because their starvation has reduced their stamina and ability to concentrate, or because they are too cold to go outdoors even in the relatively mild fall or spring weather. The self-starver also has a tendency towards isolation. If medical or psychological problems obviously make it impossible for her to attend regular school, other arrangements must be made. The starver who gets "out of sync" with her peers has one more reason to feel like a failure. Many school systems have programs for the handicapped that provide free tutoring at home and, in most such programs, a child with a psychological/medical disorder such as self-starvation qualifies as handicapped. At both high school and college levels, there are hundreds of independent study courses for credit that do not require regular class attendance. (Also see chapter 10.)

Be Patient.

Change is a great frightening dark beast to self-starvers: it is the later-life equivalent of the monster in the closet that makes small children ask for a night light. Control, after all, is what self-starvation is all about. It means that things stay the same. Change implies a loss of control. It is one of the many paradoxes of self-starving that the sufferer must give up control to gain control. She must stop attempting to control her life (and the lives of others) by starving and instead start working with it through the process of trial and error, by which the vast majority of people make their way in life. Our lives are not a perfect process; they often entail pain, but this is normal and human. The starver's form of control, on the other hand, is mechanical, obsessive, bent on total security in a chancy world, unable to accept risk and uncertainty. To perform one act as simple as eating something without knowing its exact calorie content is, for the self-starver, as terrifying as walking a tightrope blindfolded.

The steps must be small and must be taken one at a time. Parents must be prepared for some steps forward to be followed by a step backward. Progress toward recovery is hardly ever a smooth upward progression. It is more usually a series of erratic up-and-down movements leading irregularly toward the goal. It is not meant as a joke to say that dealing with a self-starver is a lot like dieting. One must only think of the pound you want to lose today and not of the fifty pounds you want to lose over the long run. With self-starvation the run may be long indeed, and thinking in terms of the year, or even two or three years, sometimes needed for therapy can be discouraging and disheartening. Most parents find that it helps to think not so much about "one day, when she is well," but more about, "Today she made one change in her routine; that's a little piece of progress."

Have a Sense of Humor.

This advice may seem not only impossible but heartless. A sense of humor, nevertheless, provides a sense of balance. It staves off self-pity and it helps prevent the self-starver from becoming a tragic heroine in the style of Camille. And laughter heals—especially when it is shared laughter. Every opportunity for the family to laugh together should be cherished as if it were precious. So should every opportunity to "lighten up" when situations become tense. It is particularly healthy for the starver for those close to her to be a little easygoing, less intense than she is. It may encourage her to try it also, which would be a significant step. As one psychologist has noted, self-starvers "just can't ever be casual."

The following is a convenient brief list of rules for dealing with the self-starver in the family:

DON'T

1. Do not feel guilty. Of course you have not been perfect parents. Family problems, however, are only part of the story in self-starvation and, in any case, what is past is past and cannot be undone. What matters is what you do *now* about your child's problem or any family problems.

2. Do not make food an issue. If your child wants to eat alone, let her. But be sure to tell her that you would like her to eat with the family, and that, if she does not, she will be missed. Tell her you hope she will soon feel like eating with the family again. Then drop it. Do not nag her about food or criticize her eating habits. Conflicts over food give her opportunities to manipulate. If she wants to cook, let her—but not all the time.

3. Do not let your concern about the self-starver take

your attention away from you marriage or your other children. Making her the center of attention rewards her self-starvation and prolongs it.

4. Do not pity her. She is already full of self-pity. Be concerned and attentive, but do not oversympathize. She needs opportunities for independence and responsibility, not coddling.

5. Do not be intimidated by suicide threats. These should be discussed with a theapist who will advise you when and how to take them seriously without being manipulated by them.

6. Do not allow her to dictate family activities or behavior or determine the family's eating, sleeping, or social schedules.

7. If your child is a binge eater, do not join her in her attempts to hide it. Let her know that you know and want to help.

Do

1. Show her by acts as well as words that you love and respect her. But make sure she understands that your life is important, too.

2. Give her every opportunity to take responsibility— but without demanding or urging.

3. Combat perfectionism. Admit your own mistakes; make no scenes or issues about hers.

4. Recognize and respect her values and ideals even if they differ from yours. Talk over the differences with her, but not as if she were just a child who "doesn't know any better."

5. Try to be patient and take each day as it comes. Recovering from an eating disorder may take a long time; if you concentrate on the distant day when she is well, the time will seem even longer.

6. Get help for yourself, through psychological counseling or a parent support group. Talk about your problem with

close relatives or friends—but respect your child's need for privacy if she expresses it.

7. Do attend to any really serious emotional or behavior problem in either parent. In particular, alcoholism has been found to have a severe negative effect on a self-starver and the affected parent *must* get help.

FIVE

IT'S ALL MOTHER'S FAULT?

So much has been said and written about the role of the mother in eating disorders that one mother stood up at a parents' support group meeting and said angrily, "Do people think all anorectics come from virgin births?" Attending such a meeting might tend to confirm such a notion: At most groups, fathers are scarce; mothers usually outnumber them by ten or twenty to one. There are many reasons for this, but the chief of them is neither that father cannot come because he is at work, nor that mother comes because it's all her fault.

It is common for professionals who study and write about eating disorders to focus heavily, even exclusively, on the mother-daughter relationship and on the mother's "contribution" to the development of the illness. Not nearly as much is written about the father's place in this history, nor is it often mentioned that fathers may be more reluctant than mothers to agree to the need for therapy or to become involved in the therapeutic process. Equally little is said or written about the mother's heavy involvement in, and contribution to, coping with the problem and trying to solve it, or of the heavy burden she bears in listening to her child, sympathizing with her, and dealing with her tantrums, demands, anger, resentment, sleep-lessness. Small mention is made of the myriad other physical and emotional tolls her daughter's problem exacts from the mother. Paramount is the agonizing dilemma faced by a mother whose instinct is to nurture, especially by feeding, but who is told by her starving daughter to "get off my back" about eating. (This message is reinforced by experienced thera-pists, who insist that eating is not the central issue and the dinner table must not be the battleground.) If the mother is unlucky, she will be told that her daughter's condition is directly related to her having coaxed her child to eat or, alterna-tively, to "watch her weight." This statement is without foundation—like nearly every assertion that makes a direct connection between a mother's act and a daughter's illness. Eating disorders are far more complicated.

Such assertions are merely one of many ways in which eating disorders are entwined with, and have contributed to, a whole mythology about mothers and daughters. It is terribly difficult to separate myth from fact in these instances, or to see where myth has influenced or created "fact." Take, for example, the notion of "like mother, like daughter"; or the notion, "If you want to know what your girl friend is going to be like in twenty years, look at her mother." Take, along with these, the ancient idea that girls *want* to be like their mothers. While this is often the case, the insistence that it is *always* true falsifies the situation in cases where it is not true, and makes the relationship between mother and daughter difficult, if not intolerable.

This is especially true when the child has an eating disorder. A self-starver and her mother are both like tightrope walkers trying to negotiate a thin wire above a canyon. The mother's challenge is to maintain a balance between the child's need for love, attention, and support and her own need for privacy, independence, respect, and free time. The daughter's footing is equally threatened by internal conflict. She wants to respect her mother and be assured that her mother has self-respect—

but she resents it when her mother behaves like an autonomous human being, a person other than just "mother." She needs firmness but resents overcontrol. She wants her mother to get her out of her fix (as mother has always done), but she also wants to be independent of her mother, to be the shaper of her own future. She fears separation, but she longs for it.

In other words, she is going through the usual adolescent conflict between reaching toward adulthood and clinging to the safety and warmth of childhood. Unlike other adolescents, however, the starver has already set into motion her own inefficient method of trying to resolve this dilemma. She has not emotionally outgrown the childhood stage where she thinks of her mother as always nurturing, available, ready to "kiss it where it hurts" and make it well. She expects her mother to kiss this hurt, too. In fact, she may depend utterly on her mother to fix it. Somewhere deep inside, she is aware that this is not the way her problems should be solved anymore. Unfortunately, she does not yet know a better way.

In such a situation, how much the mother serves as a role model for her daughter or how much the daughter resists following this model may have an important bearing on the daughter's progress and her mother's ability to communicate with her and help her.

To begin with, one of the features of self-starvation is the starver's sense—shared by many adolescent girls—that this is still definitely a man's world. Women get second best in every area. Menstruation—painful, inconvenient, unattractive—is a powerful symbol of this to those who cannot see it instead as a symbol of women's potential for creation. Such girls do not recognize the joys or rewards of womanhood or motherhood, partly because of their faulty maturation, partly because the rewards of being a man are so much more obvious, partly because of problems in identifying with mother.

In a family where the mother has tended to take a more

traditional role—as helpmate to her husband and mother to the children—where she tends to be more subservient to the father, the self-starver's belief in the second-class citizenship of women tends to be reinforced. It will certainly be strengthened in those cases where the starver does not want to follow in her mother's footsteps.

Most starvers, however, have a heightened sense of the need to be "good" and a well-developed sensitivity to what is expected of them. For this reason, they may feel they have a duty to grow up like their mothers, to emulate willingly the role model life has dealt them. This can be disastrous. For one thing, while some daughters are "born" like their mothers—meaning that they are physically similar and fundamentally of the same basic nature—others are definitely not.

Many years ago, it was common to believe that people were born with a certain nature. Such things as criminality or musical talent were thought to be handed down fairly directly from parent to child. This view later became socially unacceptable, even looked upon scornfully. It was replaced by the idea that people's personalities are largely shaped by their experiences, particularly those of childhood and the early years. To speak of somebody being born "temperamental" or "optimistic" was to invite charges of being outdated or provincial. More recently, wider acceptance has been given to the notion that at least to some degree, "biology is destiny." Biology—meaning essentially genetic inheritance—does indeed have much to do with one's personality, character, or nature. Some very recent studies of identical twins who were raised by different parents have strongly supported the view that personality is more powerfully influenced by genetics than by environment.

Certainly any mother could tell you that even a newborn has a distinct personality, that each of her children was different from birth, that you can tell within the first few days whether a baby is more likely to turn out easygoing, carefree, a good sleeper and eater, or whether the baby is going to be difficult, demanding, wakeful, and crying at night.

If the child's nature is inherently different from the mother's, it would be totally unrealistic to expect the child to try to be like her. To do so can only lead to serious frustration, disappointment, and a constant sense of failure on both sides. It is in the nature of the self-starver's personality to be particularly susceptible to this mistake and to suffer from its consequences.

Then there are cases where a child may or may not be like her mother but is very much afraid she might be. For example, if a girl thinks her mother—to use teen terminology—is "a wimp," then to be fated to be like her is an extremely dampening, if not actually alarming, prospect. A generation or two back, to be gentle, giving, self-sacrificing, and nurturing may have been the ultimate definition of womanliness. Today these attributes may be admired but may also be looked upon as soft or even spineless qualities. They do not fit the idea of liberated woman in charge of her own life, standing up for her own beliefs and rights, and "not taking any guff from anybody."

Since most self-starvers today are girls in their teens or early twenties, most mothers of self-starvers were born somewhere between the mid-1930s and the early 1950s. These were times when attitudes about men's and women's roles were still largely traditional. With few exceptions, most mothers born then grew up in families where the father was the head of the household and the mother catered to him and the rest of the family. Rather a large amount of self-sacrifice was expected of her.

This tendency toward self-sacrifice was made dramatically evident at a meeting of a parents' support group where the guest speaker was a woman psychologist specializing in helping mothers to cope with their self-starving daughters. The psychologist asked the group:

"How many of you ever take the last piece of cake or the only remaining portion of anything?"

Silence: no hands are raised. Almost every woman in the room looks surprised and uncomfortable.

"How many of you, in the last few days, have given away something you really wanted because somebody else in your family wanted it? Or given up time you had planned to use for yourself? Did you say 'It's all right. I don't mind,' even though you really did mind?"

There is a ripple of recognition and many looks of chagrin among the women in the room. The psychologist continues.

"I want every one of you to go home and make your favorite dish or cake or pie, whatever it is, and when you serve it, tell your family it's your favorite. Tell them you made it especially because you were in the mood for it, and you want the biggest piece. Or, even better still, to get away from the focus on food, plan something you really want to do—see a movie, play tennis, get your hair cut— and tell everybody your schedule for it. If anybody objects that they need you for something at that time, tell them they'll have to make other arrangements. On this occasion, you will not make last-minute changes in your plans to chauffeur anybody anywhere or sew up any hems or help with any homework. Not even if it's urgent."

The discomfort in the room is now intense. There is much twisting and squirming in chairs.

"Why is that so difficult for you?" the psychologist asks.

A few voices murmur an inaudible response. The therapist smiles sympathetically. She has conducted such sessions before and she understands perfectly that too many mothers of their generation and social level are habituated to sacrifice, to doing things for others but not having others do things for them. This kind of behavior is bad for mothers, bad for their children, and especially bad for children with eating disorders. Why?

"Your daughters have an even greater need than other young girls for a strong woman with whom they can identify, someone with a clear sense of herself, someone who is obviously comfortable and satisfied being who she is. They desperately need self-respect, and to achieve it, they need to respect you and recognize that you respect yourself. And you cannot do this until you learn to make reasonable demands of others without feeling guilty about it. I'd be willing to bet that even those of you who are able to make demands do it with an apology.

"If your daughter is to feel she has a rightful place in the world and that being a woman doesn't carry an inherent duty to be a martyr, she must learn by your acts that *you* feel you have such a rightful place. But you have to start by believing that you have a right to expect something from others, that you deserve it as much as anyone else. Just *telling* your daughter you feel that way isn't enough. In fact, if you say you feel that way but keep on behaving the way you always have, you will lose even more of her confidence and your credibility."

At first it is extremely difficult, even painful, for the self-effacing mother to start learning how to assert herself in a nonbelligerent way. Some mothers who have been told by therapists that they must begin to be nicer to themselves and expect more from their families are so uncomfortable with this concept that they go too far in the opposite direction. They cover up their discomfort with bossiness or defiance, as if to say, "Don't you dare contradict my right to ask this of you." This merely reflects their own lack of confidence concerning that right.

Such changes must be made slowly. A mother might begin by asking someone in the family to do a small task for her. (She needn't begin with the starver, but the starver must be included at some point.) The task might be as simple as making her a cup of tea or walking to the corner drugstore to buy her some shampoo. It should be a personal service to the mother, not a contribution to the family. The task should also be something in addition to each family's usual household responsibilities. And if, heaven help her, there is a mother who hasn't already assigned duties to all of her family, she'd better begin doing so immediately.

The mother's requests for services or attention should be expanded and increased gradually. At the same time, she should consider all the other ways, subtle or direct, of communicating the basic message: "I am an important person. I like and respect myself. I expect to be treated accordingly." Among practical things to do: splurge a little on an article of clothing, a new record, a night at the theatre or a matinee with a friend. If you and your husband have not been away from home for a long time, take a weekend trip. If you and your husband *always* do things together, do something by yourself for a change.

It should not take long for your family to get the message. They will be somewhat surprised. They may resist. They may even be resentful. You may overlook these responses or you may wish to deal with them directly: "I know you don't like it for your mother to change. But it's important to me. I hadn't realized how much I had submerged my self in my family. I love you all just the same, but I have now realized that loving doesn't mean giving everything up to others all the time."

Two extremely significant things will happen as a result of this endeavor. Your child will have more confidence in you, and thus more confidence that you will be able to help her and support her as she works out her problem. Equally important, you will be happier.

In other families, where the mother is independent, working successfully at a career or making a successful career of
being wife, hostess, "mistress of the house" in a positive way
(rather than simply housekeeper), different kinds of problems
may arise. The self-starving daughter of this kind of mother
may be intimidated by this role model. In these times, she
may feel as strongly pressured to follow in her mother's footsteps as young boys have traditionally been expected to follow
in their fathers'. This could be threatening and frightening to a
young girl who is trying to find out who she is. Role models
can be helpful in this process, giving the girl some secure
pattern to guide her emerging personality. But they can also
be overwhelming. As one therapist put it, "Some mothers can
be an awfully hard act to follow." The attractive, hard-work-
ing, competent, popular, successful mother can appear to a
troubled, uncertain daughter as an unattainable ideal. An insecure child may fear that any attempt by her to emulate such a
"superwoman" is doomed to failure. And failure is one of the
things that most terrifies the kind of girl who is prone to an
eating disorder.

One of the greatest allies a parent of either sex can have in
dealing with a self-starver is knowledge. The mother who
attempts to unravel the nature of her relationship with her
child, who does so in the most objective, clearheaded way,
takes the first important step toward appropriate change. It is
wise to ask yourself how your daughter sees you, whether she is
like you, wants to be like you, or the contrary. Usually, adolescent girls need reassuring, and reminding that they are *separate*
from their mother, whether they are like her or not. Starvers
need such reassurance in an even larger measure, and those who
fear being like their mother need it in unrestricted amounts.

It is also a primary task to learn from your child what she
thinks about these issues. Her perception may not be the same
as yours, and it may not even be the same as another observer's.
That does not matter. What counts is how she sees it. If her

version of your relationship is markedly different from yours, or from the way everyone else involved sees it, she needs some help in coming to a clearer understanding. She must not be directly contradicted. She can be asked: "Do you really think you're as stubborn as I am? I can't think of any examples. Can you?" If possible, the differences in perception should be brought to her therapist's attention so that they can be worked out in individual sessions with the child.

Keen observation and most of all a deeply sensitive *listening* ear can reveal much that had not previously been guessed. It also helps a parent to listen to herself (or himself). Too often, parents fall into habits of parenting that are no longer appropriate to the child's stage of life. For example, a mother's instinct to protect a small child can turn into overprotectiveness when the child is mature enough to fend for herself. This is a special danger with starvers, because their sense of competence and self-esteem is so very fragile. Listen for how often you say, "Here dear, let me help you with that," or, "You'll hurt yourself trying to lift that, I'll do it." Avoid all the endless variations of, "Don't forget to brush your teeth," "Look both ways before you cross the street," or "Don't forget your homework." Constant reminders of this kind tend to make the child rely on you to remind her or instruct her, instead of doing it herself. Forgetting to take her homework to school once or twice, and getting low grades as a result, will very quickly teach her not to forget.

Some of these instructions and reminders are necessary to teach very small children how to survive, but the responsibility should be handed over to the child at the earliest opportunity. None of the "let me do it for you" variations are ever necessary and are always to some degree destructive of the child's ability to learn competence and, with it, self-esteem. Every time a parent "rescues" a child from the frustration of a difficult chore by saying, "Here, I'll finish that for you," it robs the child of the joy of conquering difficulty. This behavior also teaches the child that the parent has no confidence in the child's ability to do anything or solve any problem. If the parent is always there to finish a tough job, pick up the pieces, let the child off the hook when things get rough, why should the child bother? Overprotective parental behavior seriously undermines a child's chances at self-sufficiency and self-respect.

The supermarket offers an opportunity for a revealing look at parental attitudes and their effect on children. Some parents encourage or expect a child to help unload the wagon at the checkout counter, pack the bags, help carry things to the car. Others do not let the child help at all or, if they do, become impatient with the child's natural slowness at these tasks and begin to snatch things from the child's hands. The effect of these two approaches on the children is remarkable. In the first case, the children are usually eager, cheerful, pleased with the excitement and satisfaction of doing and helping. In the other situation, the children are often whining, bad-tempered, and hard to control.

Coping abilities are a vital part of growing up and they are crucial to the self-starver's ability to recover. The parent who can provide the teen-age equivalent of expecting a child to pack groceries will be helping that teen-ager enormously to reach self-sufficiency and a healthy identity. It will also help her to achieve the necessary separateness from her mother. Sometimes, because of the nature of self-starvation and the mother's drive to restore her child's health, a mother may identify too closely with her child. One mother said to her therapist, "I can tell from my daughter's expression when she gets off the bathroom scales whether she's gained or lost weight. If she's gained, I know we're going to have a bad day." The therapist responded promptly and firmly, "No, it means *she's* going to have a bad day."

The underlying message in any of these examples is that a mother's main task is to provide warm and loving support and encouragement to her daughter while helping her to achieve separateness. The starver must recognize deeply and certainly that she has a life apart from her mother's, needs and wishes different from her mother's, and competence to live independently of her mother. Indeed, she needs to accept and be comfortable with the reality that sometimes her needs and wishes will conflict with those of her mother's—and that this is not a cause for feeling guilty. The unique closeness of mother and daughter in the child's early years should evolve naturally into a companionship between two adult women who share a history of love and growth and in which mutual respect has replaced the nurturing, dependent relationship of their earlier years. The mother who helps her daughter win the rich gift of selfhood will find herself in the happy situation of having raised a friend.

SIX

FATHER: THE MOST IMPORTANT MAN

Great attention has been given to the difficult role of the mother in dealing with a self-starving child, and to the suffering the mother undergoes. The difficulties that confront fathers, while of a very different nature, are no less real.

Ironically, one of the things that contributes to the father's distress is the fact that mother is given—or assumes—such a central role. Although psychologists are paying more attention to fathers, there is little evidence that anyone believes now— any more than they ever did—that mothers and fathers have equal responsibility for children. "Rather, it is still commonly assumed, either explicitly or implicitly, that mothers are the primary parent, that they have the ultimate responsibility for children, and that they should take the blame if something goes wrong."[1] This has been particularly true when it is discovered that a child has an eating disorder—because, among other reasons, the mother is traditionally the "feeder" in the family. If a child develops a disorder that's related to food, what's more logical than to blame the mother?

That may make the mother's role more thorny and relieve the father of some of the burden of guilt, but not without cost to him. When something as potentially disastrous as self-starvation comes along and the father *wants* to help, to take responsibility, to "fix" what's wrong, he may be ill prepared to do so. This can be particularly painful for men who derive much of their self-esteem from their ability to take charge, to manage things, to get things done. One father put it quite clearly: "For the first time in my life, I felt I was on the outside, helplessly looking in. My wife and my daughter were engaged in some kind of combat, against her illness and against each other, and I didn't even seem able to referee. I just didn't seem to have a place in the situation." Another father says, "I was just as eager as my wife was to help our daughter. But I didn't know how. And everything I read, and everybody I asked, seemed to talk about mothers. I couldn't find out what a father was supposed to do."

These are not unique or isolated reactions. They are common. It is not just an assumption that fathers take less responsibility for childrearing, it is a reality. There are many reasons for this, including the continued emphasis on the father as breadwinner and the belief that women are by nature intended for child-rearing and, therefore, are better at it.

In fact, there's considerable evidence that this last notion is without much real basis. A very careful examination of "nontraditional" families in which the father shared equally or even took a larger share in childrearing responsibilities showed that fathers were just as competent as mothers, and sometimes were considered—even by their wives—as being better. Wives made such comments as, "No, I don't think there is a maternal instinct. I think there is a parenting instinct. If anything, John is more in tune with them than I am"; and, "David's better with the children than I am; he has a lot more patience than me."[2]

Nevertheless the father's secondary role is not only a widespread assumption but a widespread actuality. Thus it is not surprising that fathers are given vastly less attention than mothers in the literature about eating disorders. Fathers are usually discussed in the context of family dynamics, not in terms of their individual role or their own personal involvement in the genesis of an eating disorder as mothers so often are. This approach to the father is not peculiar to eating disorders. It is pervasive in most other areas of child psychology.

For more than a century, psychological and sociological studies of child development and child-rearing have, in general, focused on the mother. This has remained true even now that the breakdown of traditional roles has in part altered the situation where fathers' energies were focused on work and the children's moral, religious, and educational development was primarily in the hands of mothers. Experts continue mainly to pursue the mother-child relationship. As Michael E. Lamb of the University of Utah has said, "the focus on mother-infant and mother-child relationships became so extreme and imbalanced that researchers were forced to ask whether fathers could legitimately be deemed irrelevant entities" in the upbringing of their children.[3] This imbalance is only now beginning to be righted.

What was overlooked, and has recently been documented by psychological and sociological studies, is that the father has a very specific and *direct* impact on children's growing up. In addition, there is a further significant *indirect* impact through the father's relationship with and attitude toward the mother.

Some of these more recent studies clearly indicate that fathers play a crucial role in their daughters' general personality development as well as in specific aspects of their development. In one such study, college girls who perceived their fathers as having been very nurturant and positively interested in them scored high on a personal-adjustment test. In contrast, students who perceived their fathers as having been rejecting scored very low on the adjustment measure.[4] Another study of college students showed that females who had long-term romantic relationships reported closer relationships with their fathers than did females who did not have serious heterosexual involvements.[5] Still another study showed that women who have successful, long-lasting marriages were more likely to have had a warm, affectionate relationship with their fathers.[6] In fact, it could be said that a father is the most important man in a woman's life, since he so powerfully influences her later relationships with other men.

A close and supportive father-daughter relationship appears to be associated with a greater degree of what psychologists call "internality" or "locus of control,"[7] meaning a sense of self-discipline from within rather than discipline that is imposed by others. This is of particular importance in the issue of children with eating disorders because they often feel overwhelmed and helpless. Indeed, for many years it has been an almost universally accepted tenet of psychology that an internal sense of values and healthy self-concern leads to greater psychological well-being rather than "correct" behavior based on external pressures or fear of punishment. Fathers who are supportive of their daughters, psychologists also agree, make it easier for the daughters to make the necessary separation from their mothers during adolescence.

Particularly interesting in the context of eating disorders is the recent acceptance by many psychiatrists of the fact that fathers have much to do with their daughters' gender identity. For many years, it had been recognized that fathers have a crucial influence on their sons' "masculinity." Recently, however, it has been demonstrated that fathers have an equal—or perhaps more important—influence on their daughters' "femininity." Moreover, fathers significantly affect the development of daughters' self-esteem, a key factor in eating disorders. The issue of femininity is particularly important in eating disorders because developing a strong identity—which means a strong female identity—is a major task for the starver.

Femininity has traditionally been defined in rather negative terms. The stress has been on docility and gentleness, peacemaking behavior, warmth, and sensitivity to the needs of others (even at the expense of self). Girls were not supposed to be aggressive, either physically or emotionally, not even in the more modern sense of simply being strong about protecting their own interests and not allowing others to take advantage of them.

Modern psychologists tend to define femininity more positively, as reflecting a feeling of satisfaction in being a woman, and including a sense of independence and the ability to be appropriately assertive as well as warm and sensitive. It entails the capacity for standing up for one's beliefs, convictions, and needs, as well as the traditional feminine inclination toward negotiation and peacemaking. This definition has much less to do with traditional feminine or masculine qualities than it does with a sense of personal wholeness, regardless of gender. However she defines femininity—whether she chooses a traditional wife-mother role, a strictly career-oriented one, or a combination of both—what makes a woman feminine is her sense of pleasure and satisfaction in being female.

Thus, the father who accepts his children for themselves, without attempting to mold them according to some ideal pattern, is most likely to contribute to the children's satisfaction with their gender role, however they define it.

A lack of acceptance can take many forms. Fathers often have more rigid sex-role stereotypes than mothers, and they may withhold approval from a child who does not precisely fit those stereotypes. Psychological studies have shown that fathers of very young children are more likely to be patient with an overactive, mischievous son than with a daughter who behaves the same way. "Boys will be boys." Fathers seem to have less difficulty accepting a "difficult" son than a "difficult" daughter. This kind of attitude makes the daughter feel rejected and contributes to her potential feeling of inferiority to the male and the sense that the world treats men better than women.

Psychologists also generally agree that fathers are more concerned about sex-role differences than mothers and that their behavior toward their children reflect this. They often fail to encourage—or may even actively discourage—physical or intellectual achievement in their daughters. This is more likely to be the case where there is no son in the family. On the other hand, the father's traditional wish to have a son may cause him to reject his daughter's femininity and, instead, encourage her to adopt more masculine traits. He may unconsciously treat his daughter like the son he never had. He may, for example, push her harder toward achievement of some kind and, in general, make greater demands on her to satisfy his need to be proud of his child. This need not mean that such a father urges his daughter to play baseball. The demand could be more subtle, like encouraging her toward a traditionally masculine profession such as law, or praising her lavishly for good grades or being elected class president while neglecting to compliment her on her attractiveness or her sense of humor. Such a father might simply be less demonstrative and affectionate toward his daughter, more aloof and stern.

Finally, some fathers, particularly older ones, are still raising their daughters as if the social changes of the last ten years had never occurred. It must be quite difficult for men who have been instilled with certain attitudes towards women to try to adjust to completely different ideas and expectations from the women in their lives. Many men are unable to do so. They continue to expect their daughters to be compliant, to speak softly, and to be polite and respectful—especially to the "head of the house." Such a father may expect the family to be run in the traditional patriarchal fashion. In such families, the mother may also be expected to remain in the traditional role of helpmate, to shoulder a larger share of household responsibility and a lesser share of important decision-making. This may create confusion and conflict in a daughter, pitting the values she is taught at home against the ones she learns outside of it. This makes it even more difficult for the emerging adolescent female to make the necessary transition from family orientation to society orientation. The shift in such cases is too drastic and imposes a greater load of guilt on her for "turning her back" on her family so sharply.

At the same time, a fundamental and paradoxical aspect of the father-daughter relationship has not changed with the changing status of women. In order to grow into a healthy woman, a girl needs affection, compliments, praise, and admiration from her father. In other words, she needs to be "romanced" in a healthy, non-incestuous way. Steven Levenkron, the developer of the nurturant-authoritative approach to treating eating disorders, has said that the failure of a father to do this is one of several contributing factors in the self-starver's typical disinterest in sexuality. (Among the others are fear of physical or emotional intimacy, and fear of parental abandonment.)[8] There are many reasons why a father might not "romance" his daughter. One is an inability to show affection and warmth, or sometimes even an inability to love. Another common reason is the father's fear of unhealthy behavior toward his daughter, which has become a more powerful concern in recent years with the widespread publicity given to incest and child sexual abuse. Incest taboos are so powerful that a father can be terrified by any feeling toward his daughter that even remotely borders on the sexual. As a result, he may put greater distance between himself and her than he really wishes.

Whatever the cause, such distance can have a very negative effect on a daughter, especially one who is prone to developing an eating disorder. Most psychologists agree that the positive effects a father is capable of having on his daughter's development depend on his having sufficient interaction with her. Thus the extent of his commitment to childrearing is crucial. If he is physically or emotionally "absent," he cannot achieve these benefits. As one psychologist has put it, "His unavailability to provide feedback to the young woman regarding her self-worth makes her more sensitive to the impact of negative influences in the culture, such as the drive for thinness, the emphasis on weight reduction, appetite control, and the view of emaciation as beautiful."[9]

In a study of thirty-nine self-starving girls, this psychologist found that thirty-six of them characterized their fathers as emotionally disengaged and believed that this distant relationship was a significant factor preceding their illness. They described their father as very self-absorbed and incapable of dealing with feelings. "This lack of input from dad often resulted in the anorexic's impression that she had not measured up to his expectations or that she was to blame for problems in this relationship or in the family. The lack of paternal support and involvement contributed to low self-esteem and later attempts to do anything, including hurting their bodies by starving, to gain attention and affection."[10] The father's absence, Dr. Margo Maine points out, does not cause eating disorders. It can, however, "compound difficulties in the mother/child relationship, in family dynamics, in developmental mastery, in self-acceptance, in psychosexual development, and in management of the cultural demands placed on young women."[11] A typical comment by one of the girls in this study was:

> I don't have any childhood memories of him—he didn't have much of an impact. He is very quiet. He didn't tell me he loved me until I was 17. That hurt me a great deal. Maybe if he had conveyed positive things to me about myself I would have been stronger and resisted all the other pressures. Instead, I felt powerless and that all men were frightening and demanding. I took it out on my body—first, trying to be thin and more attractive, then really just wanting to fade away.[12]

Almost half of the girls in this study reported that their fathers had been involved in early years and then through illness, alcoholism, or divorce, became distant. Other experts, however, have noted that this trend from closeness to distance often occurs without such dramatic causes, most often during the high school or college years. "Most women related their conflicts with fathers to their first step toward separation from the family. At this time, some fathers seemed to want them to stay little girls or, at least, to accept the traditional feminine role."[13]

A father who sees himself fitting into these descriptions may reasonably ask what he can do about it. After all, we are all the way we have become, and changing one's nature when well into maturity is not a simple task. But changes can be made. Dr. Margo Maine, who conducted the study of the thirty-nine girls, has described a case in which a noninvolved father became very successfully involved with his daughter.

The girl, age sixteen, had been in therapy for a year, but was making no progress and was physically in very bad condition. Her parents, divorced when she was thirteen, had had a very difficult marriage, constantly fighting during the rare hours her father took away from his business to be at home. After the divorce, the girl saw her father frequently, but on her mother's remarriage, her father felt uncomfortable calling or coming to see her, and their relationship broke down. The girl now felt distanced from him as well as from her mother and from her stepfather, about whom her feelings were extremely negative. Attempts at family therapy with the mother and stepfather failed, but the girl began having very productive family sessions with her father. She began to understand how much his business had meant to him and why it had kept him away from home so much. They began to identify common interests and to spend time together. For the first time in years, he took a one-week vacation with her and her sister. The girl finally realized that her step-family situation was very painful and that she felt more emotionally genuine and alive with her father.

This girl recovered fully from her eating disorder and has adjusted well in her career and her personal life. She feels more emotionally connected and real with her father, and sees his support as having been crucial to her recovery.[14] For a father to make healthy changes in his relationship with his daughter, and to help her with her eating problem, the first step is to take a good clear look at the situation and recognize the nature of the relationship and of the personalities involved. Only with a good understanding of what has been going on in the past can one begin to build a more constructive future.

One father told a support group that when he asked the family therapist what he should do to help, the therapist replied, "Be a father." The father's response was largely bewilderment. "For the first time," he said, "it struck me that I didn't exactly know what a father is, or how to be one." His reaction is not surprising. A great many fathers would probably react the same way, for a great many reasons. One is that "fathering" is not generally considered a man's most important role in life—as being a mother has been for women. Men do not derive their sense of identity chiefly from fatherhood but rather from achievement. Further, the cultural stereotype of masculinity does not include "nurturant, caregiving behavior, and an integral part of male socialization in Western societies today is the expectation that males will fulfill an instrumental role in the work force rather than an expressive role. Forms of socialization range from 'He can't have dolls, I don't want him to grow up to be a homosexual,' to 'Don't cry, Angus, be a man.' " And, finally, men who take an active part in home or child care may be seen as under their wives' thumbs.[15]

There is no evidence, however, that men are by nature incapable of parenting or that they are inferior to women in their capacity for warmth and expressiveness. The major difference between fathers and mothers in their effectiveness as parents is probably just *experience*. In our society, women are brought up, whether deliberately or unconsciously, to fulfil a mother's role. It is the girls in the family who are expected to help with the newly arrived sibling; it is the girls who earn spare money babysitting while the boys deliver newspapers. Young boys emulate their fathers in their roles as athletes, wage-earners, achievers, not as fathers. Young girls may emulate their mothers as achievers as well, but they are far more likely than boys to identify themselves with their mothers in domestic roles.

A few things a father can do to help a self-starving daughter include:

1. Consider spending more time with your daughter, particularly doing things *she* likes to do. Do you have interests in common that you haven't been aware of or have neglected? No one would suggest, for example, that you quit listening to your favorite classics and become a rock fan, but have you ever listened at all to her music? You might be pleasantly surprised. Have you, like many fathers, left to your wife the chores of attending parents' night at her school or going to see her in a school performance or athletic activity? Have you begged off seeing her perform because of the pressures of work or fatigue? Your wife is probably busy and tired, too. Children attach great importance to the attention of their parents to their endeavors and successes, and for a girl, a father's approval is especially valued.

2. Give her your approval—without her having to *do* anything to get it. A spontaneous smile, a compliment she hasn't "fished" for, any expression of affection and admiration—these may seem minor but to someone whose self-esteem is almost nil, every bit counts. Do not make her work for your praise. As one girl has said, "I had always wanted to win his approval—it may be part of why I became a lawyer. The only way to get his attention was to do something drastic. My weight loss was the only thing that ever worked in getting his concern. It still does."[16]

3.   Do not set up expectations and praise her only when she meets them; for example, do not tell her either explicitly or implicitly that you expect her to get high grades and then praise her when she does.

4.   Talk to her about yourself. Many men find it difficult to express their thoughts or feelings to others, especially to women and to the younger members of their families. One self-starver told a parents' meeting that she knew a lot about her father's ancestry but absolutely nothing about him. He was in a very real sense a stranger to her. Naturally, being as self-critical and guilt-ridden as most self-starvers, she assumed this was her fault: he did not consider her important enough or smart enough to honor her with his confidences.

5.   Learn to encourage your daughter when she wants to achieve and compete instead of trying to protect her from challenge and responsibility. This is especially important as a counterfoil to social pressures. Try to remember that women who are successful in the best sense of the term are generally those with strong relationships with fathers who encourage them to be adventurous, confident, and sure of their place in the world rather than those whose fathers fostered passivity and traditional "femininity."

6.   Reexamine your relationship with and behavior towards your wife. Are there tensions between you? Can you discuss them and relieve them? Do you feel that she has failed you in some way, and can you talk to her about it in a way that is not hurtful but instead opens up communications and the possibility of change? Can you suggest to her that she do the same? If your reexamination indicates to you that you have been treating your wife with less than full respect and affection, this is something that needs attending to. Self-starvers are especially sensitive to any sign of disrespect or contempt by the most important man in their lives towards the most important woman. If your reexamination reveals serious flaws in the partnership—especially if it reveals fundamental differences in

your ideas about how to raise children or how to deal with your child's eating problems, professional help is essential.

7. Take a good look at yourself. Are there pressures on you that leave you emotionally, mentally, or physically drained, so that you have no resources left for your family? Can you relieve yourself of these pressures? Are there frustrations and disappointments in your own life that depress you and absorb your energy? Can you help yourself overcome these or get help from elsewhere? Have you reached that stage of life where you discover you have fallen short of your youthful dreams and goals, and does this preoccupy you or make you lose interest in the other areas of your life such as family? Can you set and reach new goals, or accept the accomplishments you have achieved and stop grieving over those you lost? Can you find comfort and pride in your family instead?

8. Finally, take a good look at your daughter. What do you like about her? Tell her about it.

SEVEN

GOALS AND TYPES OF THERAPY

Practically the only aspect of self-starvation on which there is universal agreement is that therapy is vital. Undoubtedly some sufferers have recovered without therapy. One expert estimates that perhaps 40 percent of self-starvers can expect to recover naturally or else be very much improved after about six years. However, not only would those people have recovered more quickly had they been involved in some sort of therapy, but probably many of those who were only "improved" would have recovered as well.

Help is essential and it must be sought very early. Delay only allows the bad eating habits, tyrannical behavior, discouragement, low self-esteem, and feelings of failure to become more deeply embedded. At a certain point they become extremely difficult—sometimes impossible—to root out. All experts caution that the longer the history of self-starving, the harder it is to treat.

So the parents' first responsibility is to get their child into therapy. It would be nice to think that this is as simple as the sentence makes it sound. It is not. There are two major problems: the first is the difficulty of finding the right therapist, the second is that starvers notoriously resist entering treatment. (The latter problem will be discussed in the next chapter.)

Before one even begins to think about choosing a therapist, it is most important to understand something of the goals of therapy. Then one must know something about how various therapies go about trying to attain those goals. This knowledge will allow a more informed choice of a therapist. It will also make it easier to avoid therapists who either do not have the appropriate goals in mind or do not have the appropriate methods for achieving the appropriate goals.

When a starver has reached a stage where her life is threatened, the immediate priority must be weight gain. Therapists have repeatedly pointed out that weight gain alone is not a sign of recovery, but weight gain is necessary to recovery. While the starver is in a semistarved state, metabolic, neurological, and hormonal changes cause both physical and mental abnormalities that interfere with normal feeling and thinking. A person in this physical condition is in no state to attempt problem-solving tasks or to deal with the deep, complex emotional difficulties she must solve.

The ultimate goal goes well beyond a change in eating patterns. The ultimate goal is to help the starver find normal and effective ways of dealing with the problems of life. Many therapists are convinced that although a starver can be induced by all sorts of methods to change her eating habits (at least long enough to ward off imminent death), a fundamental and long-term change cannot take place until at least some of the underlying problems are resolved.

Among the important tasks that therapy should help the starver and the binge eater/purger to achieve are the following:

Acceptance and appreciation of her body in its nonstarved state. Most self-starvers think of themselves as fat or on the verge of being fat even when their bones show through the skin. Attaining a more normal "body image" is essential. Liking the image is the highest goal.

Learning to like herself: developing an identity other than "the thin one." She must discover what makes her who she is and what gives her value apart from her appearance and especially apart from this rigidly controlled, artificial identity she has bought at the high price of endangering her health and jeopardizing her future. As mentioned elsewhere, many starvers and binge eaters are simply incapable of recognizing that they have any valuable qualities other than their ability to eat less or purge more than anybody else.

Relinquishing childhood for womanhood. The starver must learn to accept her "femaleness." This means not just being of the female gender, but learning to appreciate the joys and gratifications of being a woman and learning to accept the risks and rewards of womanhood and sexuality.

Taking risks. People with eating disorders are maddeningly resistant to change, especially if they cannot predict or control the consequences. Part of giving up the unhealthy control they have over others and gaining a healthy control over themselves involves taking chances, being impulsive, and discovering that the world does not end when the results of risk-taking are unexpected or even unpleasant.

Making decisions and accepting responsibility. A self-starver may stand at a store counter for an hour trying to decide between the blue shirt and the green one. This is partly because of her deep fear of being wrong, of making mistakes, and partly because of her wish to avoid responsibility. Being able to accept herself—including her mistakes—and recognizing that making a mistake does not mean she is "a bad person" are essential to her recovery.

Learning to trust. Self-starvers cannot trust themselves. Their rigidity about eating patterns and other behavior is based on the fear that if they let themselves go they will "go whole hog." They cannot trust themselves to go just a little way and then stop. Similarly they cannot trust others. They feel they must keep their deepest secrets hidden because if they tell anyone else an intimate feeling, that person will use it against them. The starver must learn to believe that others will keep their word and respect her feelings. Thus she can learn to believe she can keep her own word and respect her own feelings.

Learning new ways of thinking. Self-starvers are often the victims of faulty or illogical thinking (which, however, they can often make sound quite logical). They are also often perfectionists and suffer from the typical perfectionist's dead-end reasoning, such as: (1) All-or-none thinking, where everything is either black or white, good or bad. "If I don't get an A in this course, I'm a failure." "If you don't agree with me about this, you think I'm wrong about everything." "If you dislike any one thing about me, you don't like *me*." (2) Dogmatic negativism: an insistence that if anything goes wrong once, it will always do so. To lapse for one moment from a strict diet means one will continue lapsing straight into the terrible, inevitable result—fat. "Last week I had a snack between meals and gained a half-pound. If I have a snack today, I will gain a half pound." (3) "Should" or "must" self-instruction. "I should do this, I shouldn't have done that, I ought to do something else." Starvers tend to make moral issues out of things with no moral content. "I must be thin because being fat means you don't have any self-control." "I must wash my hair every day because untidiness is bad." "I must keep on working without a break even though I'm tired, because stopping would be self-indulgent."

All of these kinds of faulty thinking block the self-starver's path to recovery. They can be corrected with appropriate professional guidance and family support.

Realigning relationships. Basically, this means learning to be a separate person, not merely a daughter and especially not merely a copy of mother. The starver needs to learn how to think for herself and not rely on others to tell her what she is thinking or should be thinking. She also needs to overcome the opposite tendency to reject everything her parents say just because they are her parents. She needs to find a healthy balance between overdependence and total rebellion.

Living in the present. Starvers have a defeatist way of dwelling on the past and fearfully anticipating the future, thereby neglecting the immediate moment. They dwell on past hurts, insults, rejections, and mistakes. They mistrust the future, because they have no control over it and because they believe it is doomed merely to repeat the past. Nor do they trust any evidence that they are mistaken about this. A starver can turn in ten assignments, get an A on every one, but still assume that she is going to get a D on the eleventh assignment. Starvers need to be able to leave the past in the past, to greet the future only as it arrives, and to live in the moment. They need to learn to accept and savour the "right now," to do something this minute without dwelling on what was done yesterday or postponing it for some more propitious time.

Accepting that the difficulty—and the solution—is within, not imposed from outside. Starvers often feel that they are being controlled, that God is punishing them, that they are "born losers." They feel that it doesn't matter how hard they try, they'll never succeed because they're unlucky. They must begin to accept the fact that luck is often what you make it, that even talented people do not get anywhere without hard work and determination, that few people are "lucky" or "unlucky" all the time. This acceptance can help make it possible for the starver to accept responsibility for her own recovery.

How are these goals achieved through therapy? Since eating disorders are a relatively new development, there is little agreement among professionals as to what form of therapy is best or even acceptable. Many different approaches have been tried with varying degrees of success and with varying amounts of documentation. There is thus no clear basis on which a parent (or even another professional) could evaluate the true worth of any method with much certainty. Further, professionals do not always agree on the definition of "recovery." In some cases, especially with some of the newer forms of treatment, reports of a high success rate are based on an assessment of short-term recovery only. Sometimes a therapy is called "successful" merely because it succeeds in getting the starver to gain back some weight or reach "normal" weight. Such an approach fails to take into account the need to treat the starver's basic emotional confusion. Without such treatment no results of any long-term value are possible.

In spite of this somewhat chaotic state of affairs within the therapeutic community, certain therapies can be described and to some degree evaluated. Parents may also come to some opinion about the value of different therapies by listening to the experiences of other parents.

Most people who are concerned about eating disorders have heard adverse reports about therapy. There are stories of people spending months or years getting nowhere with a therapist or of going to one therapist after another with no result beyond the waste of precious money and even more precious time and emotion. In this connection we must consider that, as a number of scientific studies have noted, there is tremendous resistance to therapy among victims of this condition. Such studies cite as proof of this resistance the many cases in which the starver has gone from therapist to therapist without result. Some of this was undoubtedly due to the victim's resistance, which, as we have indicated, is often remarkably tenacious. There is also the possibility, however, that a certain amount of this "doctor shopping" has been due to the ineffectuality of the therapeutic methods employed. Happily, such stories seem to be less common now than in the past, as therapists gain experience and learn more from the experiences of other therapists.

One may also hear horror stories of girls given psychotherapeutic drugs at random or on a "why not try it" basis. Many of the drugs are wholly inappropriate and some of them quite dangerous. Girls terrified of weight gain were given anti-depressants, which cause them to gain weight and thus become anxious and depressed. And then there are tales of girls spending their young years in and out of hospital and residential treatment centers, where they gain the demanded amount of weight and then, on discharge, go right back to starving themselves. These stories have a very real basis in fact. In the years when "anorexia nervosa" was just beginning to be recognized as a real and frighteningly widespread phenomenon, few therapists had any idea how to handle it. The record of unsuccessful attempts at therapy in those years is genuinely heartrending. Even now, when anybody who reads a magazine or newspaper or watches television has heard of eating disorders, it is still not so easy to find an effective therapist—at least not on the very first try. One must be prepared for the possibility that the first therapist will not be suitable or effective. However, there are ways parents can increase their chances of finding good therapists and of picking the best one for their child.

First it is important to know something about the various approaches most widely used.

Traditional psychoanalysis. Psychoanalysis is still being applied to eating disorders in spite of several major criticisms. Many experts consider it inappropriate because it requires the analyst to interpret the patient's reports about herself in order to help her gain insight into her behavior. Hilde Bruch notes that classic analysis, "where the patient expresses his secret thoughts and feelings and the analyst interprets their unconscious meaning, contains for patients with eating disorders elements that represent painful repetition of a pattern that had characterized their whole development, namely of being told by someone else what they feel and think, with the implication that they are incapable of doing it themselves. The profound sense of ineffectiveness that has troubled them all their lives is thus confirmed and reinforced."[1] Bruch says that the essential task of therapeutic intervention must be "offering patients assistance in developing awareness of their capabilities and potentials and thus helping them to become more competent to handle their problems of living in less painful and less ineffective ways."[2]

Another complaint is that the analyst's stance of just listening without being actively involved in communicating with the patient or moving the process forward forces the starver to carry on the conversation. Since starvers find it extremely difficult to reveal (or even to know) their inner thoughts and feelings, the analytic session often entails long periods of uncomfortable silence, during which the starver tries desperately to think of something to say so that the analyst will approve of her. If she doesn't do this to her own satisfaction, she feels a deep sense of failure and is sure the analyst does not like her because she is stupid, boring and inarticulate. This is hardly a helpful experience for someone whose basic problem is an ingrained sense of failure and worthlessness.

On the positive side is evidence that traditional analysts have helped some sufferers of starvation. It appears that in these cases the analysts have been less rigidly tied to the classic analytic method and have allowed themselves to become more actively involved in the therapy. Hilde Bruch says that self-starvers are "singularly unresponsive to traditional psychoanalysis, but 'a fact-finding, noninterpretive' approach can bring change and improvement in patients who seemed to be 'unanalysable.' "[3] She herself achieved results by "paying minute attention to the discrepancies in a patient's recall of the past"[4] and to the way the patient misperceived or misinterpreted current events, often responding to them in an inappropriate way. Such people, she explains, suffer from an abiding sense of loneliness and of not being respected. They often think they have been insulted or abused even when they have not. If the starver can be helped to explore these situations and see their reality, she can eventually learn not to experience herself as a helpless victim.

Sometimes traditional therapy works simply because the therapist happens to be "the right person" for a particular patient. Rapport, warmth, a kind of "chemistry" between therapist and starver can be even more important than the method applied. Nevertheless, since the perfect marriage of patient and therapist is not common, particularly with such therapy-resistant, wary people as self-starvers, traditional psychoanalysis seems a chancy and unpromising route.

Nurturant-authoritative therapy. This approach is a distinct departure from more traditional therapy in that the therapist takes a highly active part in the process. He instructs the patient to do certain things, pointing out where her thinking or problem-solving is ineffective, sets up certain demands and expectations for the patient, and makes promises. The therapist is firm and "authoritative" in his instructions and conversations with the starver. He is trying to give her a secure and solid structure to lean on, some limits and guidelines, and a sense that his strength will strengthen her. At the same time, he expresses empathy, concern, warmth—a "nurturant" attitude. Steven Levenkron, who developed this approach, has said that the therapist helps the starver to develop "an extraordinary trust" in the therapist so that he can then take an active role in her problem-solving efforts. This is necessary, in part, because the starver has not felt able to trust her parents to help her, seeing them as ineffective or emotionally depleted. What she requires to break through her problem is a strong person who cares deeply about her but is not crippled by excessive emotional attachment.

Nurturant-authoritative therapists agree with the view that weight gain is a necessary component of, or precursor to, recovery, and when necessary recommend hospitalization or medical treatment along with psychotherapy.

Family therapy. Family therapists assume that either the disorder arose out of some problem or dynamic within the family, that the solution is best found within the family, or both. Much, perhaps too much, has been written about "the anorectic family." What makes this surprising is that the families of self-starvers encompass a wide variety of personalities, styles of functioning as families, and marked differences in family history and the child's place in that history. In some families the parents are close and supportive, in others, distant. Families of starvers include those with mothers who work of necessity, those who work from choice and are making a career, and others in which the mother is happy and satisfied to be wife and mother only. Some families are intact while others are broken by divorce or death. There are also families in which one or both parents are alcoholics or drug abusers, while other families have no such problems. Discipline can be either firm or relaxed, parents either religious or not. This personal impression of great variety in the configurations of starvers' families is reinforced by the fact that the experts' descriptions of the "typical anorectic family" also differ from one another.

However, there is considerable support for the view that family dynamics are a factor in the development of eating disorders and even more evidence that parents have a major role to play in the recovery process. Indications of the effectiveness of family therapy make it stand up well among the various current approaches.

As in all kinds of therapy, the experience and skill of the therapist are crucial. No therapy is any better than the practitioner who applies it. One hears, for example, inexplicable stories of families sitting through session after session during which various members are asked seemingly irrelevant questions, the aim of which is never clear to them. Sometimes they are truly aimless. Even if the questions have real pertinence, if the participants do not understand their utility, little learning or growth can result. One parent told of a series of sessions with a therapist in which the major topic of discussion was why the father had never gotten a driver's license. The father eventually became hostile at what he perceived was not only unwarranted but irrelevant criticism. The other family members were baffled and annoyed by what they felt was a complete waste of time. The therapist felt he was not required to explain his aims, that he knew what he was doing and should be trusted in his pursuit of his goal, whatever it might be. In fact, his aim had been to uncover the father's tendency toward "avoidance," especially the avoidance of responsibility, which the therapist viewed as a kind of model for his daughter's avoidance of *her* responsibility to grow up. Unfortunately, the therapist's failure to make this understood by the family led not to insight but confusion.

A skilled therapist with a solid understanding of the family dynamics in eating disorders can achieve good results with family therapy and can help both family and starver to see how their behavior and relationships can be modified in healthy ways. Poor conflict-solving, for example, is common in families of children with any kind of behavior problem, including self-starvation. There are special techniques for improving conflict resolution that can be learned through the family therapy approach.

Assuming a skilled therapist, the success of this kind of therapy depends a great deal on how willing the family is to spend the time and effort involved. Even more important is whether the family members are supportive of each other and whether they are willing to be open, candid and mutually respectful.

Behavior modification. Behavioral therapy is a rather broad term that can mean a number of things. In the treatment of eating disorders, it may refer to a long-term approach to changing the bad eating habits, disruptive behavior, and self-destructive activities of the starver by helping her learn new behaviors. It is not concerned with a deep understanding of the reasons for the behavior. The underlying theory is that healthier behavior will result in healthier feelings. A particular form of behavior therapy is widely used in the treatment of acute life-threatening situations to bring the starver's weight up to a point where her physical condition no longer interferes with her ability to cope with her underlying problems.

This treatment generally takes place in a medical hospital, psychiatric hospital, or residential treatment facility. First the emergency situation must be handled medically. If the starver is in danger of imminent death, or if she refuses to eat, she is usually fed through a vein, sometimes directly through the vena cava. When the vital signs and clinical symptoms indicate physical stability, the starver is taken off medical treatment and behavior modification begins. In general, this involves a system of rewards and punishments. The starver may be placed in a room with little or no furniture, with no books, radio, television, or company. She is expected to eat a specified amount and to gain a certain amount of weight during a given period. For each weight gain, she is given an amenity—perhaps a book, then later a visit from another patient, then a radio or television set, a walk outdoors, or permission to join in recreational activities with other patients.

Behavior-modification therapy claims a high success rate, and this appears to be correct in terms of short-term restoration of weight. In-hospital behavior modification is a resource in life-threatening situations. There is a general impression among many therapists and families, however, that starvers treated by this approach may cooperate in order to gain their release but go back to strict dieting as soon as they are out. A sizeable number of them return for retreatment or find more lasting solutions elsewhere. Critics of the behavioral approach contend that treatment of the weight problem without a substantial change in thinking and feeling does not lead to a permanent recovery. They also contend that the method is too manipulative, punitive, and humiliating for a person who is already bereft of self-esteem and already too much controlled by others. These critics say the mechanistic nature of this approach may even cause worsening of the condition, because it confirms the self-starver's belief that she cannot control her own life—and that everyone else believes this, too.

In many experts' view, therapy can be effective over the long term only if it encourages the patient's capacity for personal growth and strengthens her resources for living.

Psychopharmacological therapy. In recent years, psychiatric research has produced persuasive evidence that many psychological and emotional problems have a biochemical/genetic basis or, at least, component. In several forms of psychiatric illness, application of this knowledge has led to effective treatments with drugs. Extending these findings to eating disorders, therapists have tried a variety of medications, the latest of which is a drug that appears to reduce food craving in binge/purgers. These therapies have not been in use long enough for a final evaluation, but many specialists in eating disorders apply the same criticism to drug therapy as they do to behavior modification. It is a "cosmetic" or "mechanistic" treatment that may seem to alleviate certain symptoms but has no effect on basic conflicts and confusion. Reports from parents' groups suggest that drug therapy introduces one more deleterious element in an already sadly complicated situation. They say that the drugs have side effects with which the starver must cope while already overwhelmed with other coping chores, that they sometimes cause mental confusion or apathy, and that much time can be wasted trying one drug after the other and having to wean the patient from each one. One parent said that her child was given so many different drugs, in succession or concurrently, that she was in a state of metabolic and emotional chaos. This is not evidence that drug treatment in itself is harmful, merely that drug therapy has been wrongly used. The general impression is that drug therapy should be approached with even more caution than any other treatment.

The Alcoholics Anonymous model. A number of therapists, acting on the assumption that self-starving and binge eating have much in common with other addictive behaviors, have successfully applied the AA approach to the treatment of eating disorders. The self-starver is addicted not so much to a substance or a habit but to the illness itself. The AA approach focuses on healthy attitudes and behavior, and its "one day at a time" philosophy directly addresses the starver's problem of dwelling on the past and fearing the future. It substitutes positive ideas and goals for self-destructive, negative ones. The AA method may have one drawback in tending to confirm and reinforce the starver's tendency to rigidity, but it is supportive and caring and may help a great deal toward the development of a sense of self-worth. It is probably most effective among those who feel positive toward group activities and among those who are comfortable with the somewhat inspirational or semireligious tone of the AA model. Certainly this approach is a promising possibility for those starvers who also have a drinking or drug problem.

Hospitalization for medical emergencies. Parents of a self-starver who is in therapy should discuss with the therapist such matters as what signs of medical danger to watch for and when to call the therapist for hospitalization or when to take the child to the hospital themselves. Parents whose child is not in therapy but is rapidly losing weight or losing alarming amounts over a longer period, should be knowledgeable about which nearby hospitals have special units or physicians skilled in handling the medical problems of starvation. Anorexia associations and parents' self-help groups can usually supply this information. Alternatively, parents should inquire about such facilities at the nearest medical-school affiliated hospital. If there is none within a short distance from home, any nearby hospital could handle an immediately life-threatening situation, but the child should be transferred as soon as possible to a specialized unit or institution.

Ideally, hospitalization for an emergency should entail not only medical attention but should also deal with the psychological and emotional problems during the recovery period. In specialized units, the starver is more likely to receive supportive and sensitive care, such as that described at St. George's Hospital, London. There, the patient

> is assured that, though in bed, eating a normal diet and gaining weight at the rate of one and a half kg [a little over three pounds] a week, first, she will be protected from overeating, and second, no one is going to tell her that she "looks well" when she has gained weight (on the contrary, the staff will recognize that, at this stage, she will feel more sustainedly chaotic, terrified and despairing than ever), and third, she will be involved in intensive psychotherapy directed at her need to cope first and foremost with her refound body shape; the need for herself and others to come to see her as more than merely this body shape, and her need to develop new coping mechanisms.

During the hospitalization in this institution, "all staff seek to befriend the patient . . . allowing a rich range of potentially healthy identification."[5]

Hospitalization for non-emergency treatment. Until recently, hospitalization for eating disorders took place chiefly in psychiatric facilities or residential treatment centers. There the starver might be placed with other patients with a variety of conditions, including schizophrenia, alcoholism, sociopathic behavior, suicidal tendencies, drug abuse, and the like. It takes no psychiatric expertise to conclude that such company is obviously unsuitable for a child with an eating disorder, and to be thrust into such a situation could be extremely damaging for a child whose need is to feel normal, accepted, admired, not "weird," "crazy," or ostracized. Some therapists have gone so far as to say that *under no circumstances* would they admit a self-starver to a psychiatric hospital (and in fact would admit a starver to a medical hospital only if she were in medical danger). More recently, many of the best medical centers have set up special units for eating disorders that place the child only with others who share her condition. Patients in these centers have the attention of staff who are trained to care for their problems, as well as the advantage of group therapy sessions with others who know and understand how they feel. (A partial list of such centers is in chapter 10.) When such units are supervised by experienced, caring therapists and trained, caring staff, they can achieve good results in a shorter time than individual or group outpatient treatment. Some therapists feel that part of their effectiveness stems from simply removing the starver from the environment where her condition arose and was continuing, where she was still under influences and pressures that interfered with recovery. Others feel that in-hospital eating-disorder units provide the security and structured activity the starver needs to make her feel safe enough to start changing her life.

Some experts believe that hospital care is potentially successful only if the self-starver is suffering the kind of crisis unique to this illness: she feels she is about to recover but cannot face the enormous change this will mean to her—cannot face the loss of what has been the central focus and activity of her life. At such times, hospitalization can provide the shift in circumstances and the support that may help her make this last wrenching move toward normal life.

The same difficulty of evaluation applies to all therapies mentioned here. It is interesting that the participants at a major conference sponsored by the Center for the Study of Anorexia and Bulimia in New York entitled "Therapy for Eating Disorders: What Works, What Doesn't, and Why" agreed at the end of the seminar that the question of the right therapy remained unanswered. Scientific assessment of therapeutic outcomes is extremely difficult, and so far, no one has published any carefully controlled, large-scale, long-term studies of any particular therapy or comparison of the results of different therapies.

One clear consensus that did emerge from the New York meeting was that each therapist and each approach to therapy has to deal with a starver as a specific, highly individual case. What works for one may not work for another. What works for one at some stages of therapy may not work for the same one at other stages.

It is encouraging that people in the field of eating-disorder therapy and research are beginning to study the outcome of treatment in a scientific way. It will take a while for these studies to be evaluated or even to be meaningful, because in order to do long-term follow-up of results, scientists must study people who began treatment at least five years ago, preferably longer. This means they must include many people who were being treated by trial and error in the days when practically nothing was known or understood about these conditions. Studies of more sophisticated, codified therapies that are beginning now will not be meaningful for several years. Eventually, it can be hoped, there will be some direct evidence to help parents find the best and most suitable treatment for their child.

It is encouraging that such a meeting as the one in New York could attract hundreds of therapists from all over the country. Five or ten years ago, attendance might have been only two or three. It is also encouraging that many medical schools, psychiatric training centers, and hospitals are setting up intensive training programs for new therapists. Parents confronted with a self-starver in the family today have a vastly greater number of sources of effective help than parents of those children who composed the first wave of "the epidemic."

This is not to say that the search for the best source of help for your particular child will be brief or easy. One of the best ways to begin is to consult one of the many national and local groups that have been formed in recent years (see chapter 10).

All of them have names of local therapists who specialize in treating eating disorders. They will not recommend any particular therapist, but their lists will include specialists about whom the group has some knowledge or experience. The only way you will be able to find out anything specific about any particular therapist is to meet the therapist or to meet someone who has had experience with that therapist. A parents' self-help group is one good source for evaluations of therapists. (Information about these should be available from the organizations listed in chapter 10 or from local or county agencies that provide information on self-help groups.) Most parents who are regular participants are usually very willing to share information about the particular personalities and approaches of the therapists they have known.

A great deal of analysis and discretion may be required. An enthusiastic endorsement from a parent whose child has had a good experience with a therapist is a helpful starting point but does not necessarily mean your child will have the same experience. One clue to whether your child will be comfortable with a particular therapist might be the other parents' description of their child. Does her case sound similar to your child's? Another favorable indication would be that you feel a sense of closeness or rapport with those parents. The obvious limitation to this approach is that a therapist who sounds good to *you* might not be acceptable to your child. You can ask yourself a number of questions: Does my daughter usually like the people I like? Who is her favorite friend or relative and what is this person like? Among teachers, does she seem to like those who are strict but from whom she has learned a lot, or does she prefer those who are friendly but undemanding? If the therapist under consideration is a man, it can be helpful to examine the child's relationship with her father. If it is a warm and close relationship and she loves and admires him, then a therapist who is much like her father might be a good choice. If her relationship with her father is distant or hostile, then a therapist who is unlike her father might be more appropriate. The same examination of the mother-child relationship can be useful if the therapist is a woman.

If the family physician is knowledgeable about eating disorders, you may want to ask him for a recommendation.

However armed with names, details, and recommendations you may become, eventually you will have to decide which therapist to "try out." If you have chosen family therapy, parents, child, and siblings all go together for the first visit. If you choose individual therapy, you will have a dilemma even before you start. Who goes to the first visit?

Many people feel that parents should meet the therapist first before making an appointment for the child. If you take an instant dislike to the therapist or fail to get a feeling of confidence, your daughter might also. It is not worth taking a chance that she will react negatively, thus acquiring a wonderful excuse to back out of therapy altogether. You can at least talk with one or two more before deciding. Some therapists, in fact, require a visit with the parents first. Others prefer not to see a parent first because it could give the starver the impression that the choice has been made for her and that she has no say in the matter, or that her parents and the therapist are plotting against her. The starver may believe that you have told the therapist terrible things about her and that therefore the therapist is already prejudiced against her. Perhaps the best solution to the problem is an arrangement preferred by many therapists: both parents (or parent) and child come together on the first visit. Thus, nobody "gets there first," nobody can "say anything behind somebody else's back." Except in the case of family therapy, this first session will not probe deeply into family dynamics or the personalities of the parents. It will focus largely on the therapist's getting a general history and background of the child's problems and on the parents' getting a general description of how the therapist intends to proceed. Often the therapist will have the parents in the room only for ten or fifteen minutes, then will ask them to wait outside while the child remains. This is an effective technique for immediately establishing the understanding that this therapy belongs to the child, not the parents. The parents are included to a very limited extent and they may not interfere beyond that limit. This technique emphasizes that the child is to have privacy: her confidences to the therapist will remain confidential.

Of course, the decision as to who comes to the first visit is not yours alone. Many therapists allow the parents to decide, but most have their own methods and rules. What these are should be established when you call for the appointment.

Parents not only should feel free to ask questions of the therapist, they must do so at the beginning to ensure that no misunderstandings arise. A responsible therapist should be willing to discuss in general terms how he or she approaches the counseling of a self-starver. You should also discuss specifically what your involvement will be, if any. The therapist may be among those who prefer to have no communication with the parents once therapy begins. If this is the case, you should have a clear agreement about whether you are allowed to call the therapist when a major problem arises at home, or whether he will at least give you a brief progress report from time to time. You may ask for a general idea of how long therapy may take. You are not likely to get an answer until the therapist has met with your child at least several times, but you are entitled at some point to some kind of estimate. You should discuss fees specifically and, if you have financial problems, whether the therapist uses a sliding scale based on ability to pay, or whether you can pay the fees over a period of time. Be sure to find out the rules for canceling appointments. Some therapists charge for an appointment if it is not cancelled twenty-four hours ahead; some require a week's notice. You also should ask if there are any patients or patients' parents who would be willing to talk on the phone, in strict confidence, about their experience with the therapist.

Your therapist may not be willing to give such information because of the confidential relationship between therapist and client, but it does no harm to ask.

It is essential that you ask all the questions you have. You will be spending money—possibly large amounts of it—but even more important, you and your child will be spending time. You don't want to waste any on the wrong therapist, and you don't want your child to have a bad experience that may make her reluctant or unwilling to try again. Furthermore, going through the discomfort, even pain, of telling a therapist about her problem is not something any starver wants to repeat. Young people are on a schedule, whether you or they like it or not. In this culture, finishing high school at seventeen or eighteen and going to college immediately afterward, graduating by twenty-one or twenty-two, is the norm. The starver who falls behind her peers in this schedule because of time wasted in unsuccessful therapy is going to feel even more of a failure than ever. It is always best for the starver to continue with school or work while getting therapy. Some starvers, however, cannot keep up with regular school work because of their physical or emotional condition. Alternative opportunities are available (see Chapter 10).

It is crucial for parents to understand when their child enters therapy that the path to recovery will be neither straight nor smooth. There will be periods of good progress interspersed with periods of apparent backtracking or even major relapses. This is to be expected, but it may take a major effort on the parents' part to remain hopeful and determined during bad periods and to help the child to remain so. One way of keeping perspective is to compare your child's behavior—when she seems to have taken a backward step—not with her behavior of yesterday, when she seemed to be improved, but with her behavior in the period before she started therapy. The perspective will be much clearer.

An especially difficult period often occurs when the starver panics at her first weight gain. The starver who has been no more than a collection of bones and who gains five or ten pounds and begins to look a little human may encounter an acquaintance she has not seen for some time, and be greeted with "You look so much better!" The starver translates this as, "You've gained weight," which in turn translates into, "You're fat." Even without these external triggers, the starver may panic if she feels she is regaining weight too fast, especially if she continues trying to wear the same clothes she wore at her lowest weight. Starvers have an uncanny way of playing mean tricks on themselves to set themselves up for a fall (the subconscious motive is to prove how right she was in the first place about being a born loser). For example, a starver who has gained back a moderate amount of weight may decide to dig out the blue jeans she wore two years ago when she was at a relatively normal weight. She will fall into a state of terrible despair when they are too small, regardless of the fact that two years ago she was three inches shorter and wore correspondingly smaller clothes. It might be wise to get rid of all clothing worn before the starving began and when it was at its worst— but not without your child's permission.

There is also a difficult and frightening period that psychologists call "the crisis of recovery." This may occur when the starver is on the verge of a final move toward normality and appears to be almost ready for therapy to end. Suddenly she may enter a stage of terrible desperation. This is caused by her finally beginning to confront reality and to recognize that she must give up her illness entirely in order to live a full life. At this point she feels somewhat like someone who sees the firemen holding a safety net below the window of the burning building in which she is trapped. She knows that she must jump into the net to save herself, but the jump is frightening all the same.

Alert parents should be able to recognize this phase by certain changes in the child's mood and behavior. She may have been reasonably cheerful, hopeful, more like her prestarvation self than at any time during therapy. Then she becomes depressed and anxious. Sleep patterns may change. She may become more aloof and silent. If she has been attending therapy sessions regularly and on time, she may begin arriving late or not at all. While previously she had seemed to be benefiting from the therapy and speaking of it in positive terms, she may now begin to deny that the therapy has been of any use at all. She may refuse to acknowledge any of the improvements in mood and behavior that are obvious to everyone else. She may even suddenly announce that she is stopping therapy, saying such things as: "The therapist isn't helping me any more," "It's a waste of money," "The therapist says mean things to me," "The therapist doesn't like me any more, so we're not going to get anywhere." She may say she's not going back because she is cured. A knowledgeable parent will have no difficulty recognizing the untruth of these remarks.

It is a time when parents need more patience and strength and the starver needs more support and encouragement than ever before. A close relationship between parents and therapist can be extremely valuable at this stage. Parents may feel a deep sense of frustration and hopelessness at what appears to be a cessation of progress. They may feel that all their efforts and suffering have been wasted, that they have watched and encouraged each slow step of their child's movement toward health only to see it blocked just as it was about to succeed. Parents will need to exert every effort to remain determined and optimistic and to convey this sense to their child. An experienced therapist will recognize the crisis probably before the parents do. He will know how to deal with it and to make the effort that will carry the starver right over this last fence. Nearly every recovered starver that this author has talked to has said,

"When I felt worse than I had ever felt before, that's when I really began to get better."

What makes it possible for parents to survive this period is knowledge of other people's experience that this last seemingly insurmountable hurdle is surmountable and is the last. Beyond it is a child restored to her real self and ready at last to live.

EIGHT

THERAPY: GETTING THERE IS HALF THE BATTLE

Ideally (and this has occurred in many cases), when parents are worried about their child's overzealous dieting, one or both of them can sit down and talk to her about it. They can express concern and sympathy and elicit from the child some indication that she, too, feels that things have gotten out of control. With a warm and trusting relationship between parent and child, this kind of communication may be all that is needed to initiate therapy. It may not be difficult to persuade her that although you can give her love, encouragement, and support, you cannot give her the expert help she needs. The child may readily accept—even welcome—professional intervention.

It is vital from the outset to establish a clear understanding of the situation. You, as parents, are there to provide love and support. She, however, is the one with the problem. She will be given all the professional help she needs along with your love and support, but the solution to her problem will be *hers.* The underlying messages should be unmistakable. First, she is responsible for her own life. Second, when she overcomes her problem she will have the happy knowledge that she did it herself. Then again you must assure her of your support; she will not be left to swim alone in those deep waters.

Unhappily, the quiet loving conversation that leads to ready acceptance of professional help is not the usual experience. More often the starver's resistance is so strong that she will pull out every trick in her parent-manipulation bag. She will be pathetic, defiant, or threatening; she may even make suicidal remarks. Alternatively, she may become eminently reasonable and with persuasively calm logic try to convince you that this is a problem she can solve without the trouble and expense of therapy (a point she will emphasize in particular if she knows therapy will strain the family's finances).

In order to deal with this antitherapeutic stance, it is important for parents to understand why there is so much resistance. The simple explanation is that the idea of therapy terrifies the starver.

First, she is terrified of revealing her inner self, of letting a stranger know how despicable and unlovable she is (in her belief). Lacking trust in herself or anybody else, she certainly would not trust the therapist to hear these secrets without despising her or using the secrets against her. This is especially true for binge/purgers, who have been known to describe their gorging and vomiting as "my dirty little secret."

Second, she is terrified of being cured. This is not as paradoxical as it sounds. To the nonstarver, it is inconceivable that anyone would *want* to continue suffering constant denial of food and all the other painful concomitants of this condition. In one sense, the starver feels the same way. She hates the tyranny exercised over her by her fear of fat and she hates the tyranny it makes her exercise over others. She is heavily laden with guilt over this. Nevertheless, she is terrified of being cured, because the illness has become the central fact of her life, her identity, her reason for being, her everything. The illness has become "who she is." If it is taken away from her, what will be left? What will she be? What will make her special when she isn't the thinnest girl in town?

It takes an extraordinary amount of parental skill and support to communicate a genuine understanding of and respect for the starver's fear and to assuage that fear as much as possible. It is necessary to reassure her that therapy will not make her fat and that the therapist is going to be a needed friend, not a threatening enemy. It may not be possible to persuade her of all or even any of these things, but some effort to do so will help support the other methods of getting her to seek professional help.

How hard it is to get the starver into counseling depends on a great many factors including the family structure, the degree of the starver's openness and trust, and the severity of the starver's commitment to thinness. Most directly, however, it depends on the child's age. It is generally much easier to overcome the resistance to therapy of children under fourteen. Under fourteen is also the commonest age for the onset of self-starving. At this stage, teen-age rebellion has not yet begun or at least not yet reached its zenith, and parents have considerably more control over their children's behavior and general activity. The child is still in the habit of obeying at least most parental rules and—certainly not least important—parents are in a better position to bargain or, if need be, to threaten. With a child under fourteen, parents can "simply" tell their child that she needs to see a specialist who knows how to help people who diet too strenuously. Then the parents must make a definite appointment for a day very soon afterwards.

Any resistance to this parental "suggestion" *must* be met by kind but firm insistence. The child should be told the appointment has been made and that she is expected to be ready. There can be no wavering or hesitating, no postponement of the appointment, no equivocation. The parents must present a united front. If either parent softens or weakens, the child is going to feel more insecure. What is worse, she may take advantage of the difference of opinion between her parents and play them off against each other. This play may then lead to quarrels between the parents or the three-way conflict which psychologists call "triangulation."

If one parent usually tends to overprotect or oversympathize with the child, that parent must make every effort to overcome the tendency to give in, especially if the child tries to soften that parent up with tears, pleading, or threats to withhold love. The reality here is that the child is not going to stop loving a parent who is firm and exhibits conviction and a sense of purpose. On the contrary, she is going to be reassured by the parent's strength and relieved that she has a parent who cares enough about her to protect her from herself and who is confident and strong enough to see to it that she gets needed help.

It is tremendously important for parents to convey a clear sense of confidence to the child. It's good to remember at all times when dealing with starvers that their major emotion is fear. Any sign of weakness and uncertainty is a clear signal to the child that she is not in good hands, that her parents are not strong enough or wise enough to help her. Her fear intensifies, it escalates to panic. This then is translated into a stronger refusal to cooperate in seeking therapy. Parents must not give in at this point, no matter what weapons the child aims at them (and they can be formidable). As one noted therapist puts it, "in such confrontations, if the child wins, she loses."

A few starvers welcome therapeutic intervention; most do not. The degree of resistance also depends in part on how much the eating disorder has developed, that is, how long the child has been starving and how much weight she has lost. In any case, it is always dependent on how parents handle the subject of therapy.

With the early starver, who has lost more weight than appears healthy or desirable but not yet developed other symptoms (cessation of menstruation, emaciation, excessive body hair, extreme sensitivity to cold), the parental approach might be to express concern about her weight loss and to suggest seeing the family doctor "just to check up." Depending on the degree of openness of the relationship between parents and child, this may be expressed as a general, mild concern with her nutritional state or it may be clearly stated as a concern that the child may be on the verge of becoming anorexic. In either case the expression should be one of loving interest in the child's health. There should be nothing in the approach that could be seen by the child as criticism, nosiness, or fear.

Do not suggest an appointment with your pediatrician or family doctor unless you are certain that the physician is familiar with eating disorders. If you have no way of knowing (from friends who have daughters with similar problems, for instance), then ask the doctor directly. It has been a common and sometimes almost disastrous occurrence for a family physician to say, "Oh, there's nothing wrong with her; all these young girls are on diets these days." Thus lulled into thinking everything is fine, parents look the other way. The next thing they know, they have a genuine starver on their hands.

A knowledgeable pediatrician or family physician should be able to recognize incipient self-starvation (and certainly should be able to diagnose the overt condition). He will recommend that the child see a therapist.

This is one way of easing the child into the idea of therapy and of having the first suggestion come from a professional whom the child already knows and trusts. Sometimes such a suggestion is taken more positively from someone other than parents. If, however, you are not confident about your family doctor's expertise in this area, or if your child does not have a close and trusting relationship with the family doctor, then this encounter should be avoided.

If the condition has sneaked up on everybody, has remained unrecognized until the child is markedly underweight, the approach might need to be a little different. You begin talking to the child about getting help in a calm, loving, but matter-of-fact way. If you encounter serious resistance, you may find it necessary to tell the child that she must get therapy because if she doesn't she might die. This may be unavoidable if there is severe resistance from a child who has lost as much as 30 percent of her body weight (for example, if she is five feet tall and has dieted down to seventy pounds).

It is essential that you make clear to the child exactly what the purpose of therapy is. The purpose is not to make her gain weight. The self-starver's fear of fatness is so overwhelming that she will be severely threatened by the idea of therapy if weight gain is the emphasis. She must understand that the purpose of therapy is to help her stop suffering and live a normal life. It will help her deal with her terror and her hunger. A wise and experienced therapist will assure her from the onset that she will not be forced, or even allowed, to gain too much weight, only what is needed for health. She should be assured that successful therapy will allow her to keep her weight at a healthy, attractive level without painful restrictions. It is useful for the parents to give such assurances if the child is frightened by the mention of professional intervention.

Some therapists suggest that when parents talk to their child about getting help, they should refer to it as "counseling" rather than "therapy." This accomplishes two things. First, it removes some of the threatening or embarrassing connotations associated with psychiatry. Second, it carries the clear implication that the child is going to get advice and guidance to help her solve her problem. It does not imply that somebody else is going to "cure" her or do something to her.

It is recommended that the parent or parents attend the first session with the starver, or at least they accompany her there. However, after the first few visits, most therapists recommend that the child, if she is old enough and if it is possible, should go to her appointments alone. This action will also emphasize that the problem is *her* problem and that the solution to it will be *her* solution.

Once you have agreed on the need for help, consult her about a time when she would like to have an appointment. If she postpones giving a definite answer, or hedges, or keeps changing her mind, go ahead and make an appointment, using you best judgment about her convenience. Avoid times when you know she has plans or times that are usually special for her. For example, if she likes to be in her room to read or listen to music right after she comes home from school, do not make an appointment for that time. This lets her know that although you insist on counseling, you consider and respect her feelings and needs and are not going to walk all over them. It also decreases the number of excuses she can invent for not keeping the appointment.

Once you have made an appointment, do not announce it too far in advance—more than a week—or too close to the time—less than a day. If you announce it too early, the child will have too much time to worry, to anticipate the pain she is sure she will suffer, or to imagine in detail all the horrendous things she is sure the therapist will say, do, and be. If you announce it too close to the time, she will feel rushed, overpowered, and crowded. Try to be as matter-of-fact about the time as you would about any other appointment. Be prepared to thwart any last-minute maneuvers that will make you too late to get to the appointment. This may entail attention to such details as making sure *all* her clothes are clean, pressed, and mended, so that she cannot claim she has "nothing to wear." Try to remember if there were other occasions when she dawdled and evaded and what tactics she used then. Try to think of ways to counteract or prevent them. Do not leave anything important (such as getting gas for the car) until the last minute. A starver can be incredibly clever at turning such things to her purpose. Then she will point out that it was not her fault you were late.

Remember she is not doing any of these things just to frustrate you. She is *scared.* She feels that going to a therapist is like walking off a cliff. It is not surprising that she should do anything she can to postpone the confrontation, preferably permanently.

In spite of the general and absolute rule that honesty is not just the best policy with self-starvers but the only policy, there are times when subterfuge of a minor sort is acceptable, even necessary. If you suspect that your child will be able to use delaying tactics to the point where you will miss the appointment, and nothing short of picking her up bodily will get her out of the house on time, you may want to announce the appointment as being fifteen minutes—or even a half hour— earlier than it actually is. This is not a suggestion to be considered except in desperation. Even small deceptions such as this, if discovered, can seriously undermine your child's confidence in you, erode her already fragile sense of trust.

If somehow you are outwitted by the stalling game—or by feigned illness, hysteria, or temper tantrums—you simply make another appointment and make it clear to the child you are not going to let her get by with it twice. You must make it clear that your insistence comes from your love and deep concern with her happiness and health and that your resolve is firm. You may have to back your firmness up with a threat that you will remove certain of her privileges or curtail her activities unless she complies.

When the day comes and you detect dawdling and evasion, keep calm. Do not nag or keep looking at your watch in front of your child. Do not call her attention to the time every few minutes. Above all, do not lose your temper. Your child needs support not guilt, encouragement not criticism. About fifteen minutes before time to leave, quietly remind the child that you expect to leave in fifteen minutes.

In most cases, these tactics will work. If the child is extraordinarily stubborn, if the parents are intimidated, if one parent caves in under the child's pleas or manipulation, they may not succeed. Parents may have to invent their own tactics or fall back on less attractive methods such as a strong-arm approach that will make everyone involved uncomfortable and may arouse severe resentment.

Parents must understand that if they are not willing to try practically anything to get their child into therapy, they may have to waste years living with the unresolved problem of self-starving. They may one day find themselves rushing to the hospital with a child on the verge of death. I am not exaggerating or being melodramatic in order to make an impression. This does happen.

Sometimes where parents cannot succeed, someone else can. You may want to enlist the aid of the child's best friend, a specially loved aunt or cousin, an admired and trusted teacher or clergy person. Occasionally one may find a therapist who is willing to make that extra effort to telephone the starver or even to make one house call to get things moving. Quite often recovered starvers will telephone or visit; there is considerable eagerness among these young women to help others out of the terrible prison from which they have been fortunate enough to escape. Support groups, listed in chapter 10, can often supply the names of such people in your area. A word of caution, however. If you seek help from a recovered starver, it should be someone who has returned to relatively or completely normal weight. The self-starver, meeting someone who is thinner than herself, may not be helped but rather triggered into a more intense wave of dieting, since it is the starver's goal always to be thinner than anybody else. Conversely, she should not be approached by a recovered starver who is even slightly over-weight. She will leap to the conclusion that recovery means getting fat.

None of these methods is guaranteed. But every possible method must be attempted.

It cannot be said too strongly that a child who develops this condition in the early teen years, and whose condition is recognized early, is "lucky." The chances of her getting into therapy are immensely better, the outlook for recovery considerably brighter, and the length of therapy may be significantly less than would be the case with an older daughter. When the starver is beyond the teen years, and especially if she is financially independent of the family or living away from home, everything becomes more difficult. The older starver may be more amenable to logical discussion and to acceptance of her own responsibility for her recovery, but on the other hand, parents have far less leverage with the older child. Her response to suggestions about her condition may well be, "I'm over twenty-one and I can do what I please with my life." This is quite true. Nevertheless, it does not in the least diminish the parents' sense of concern and anxiety about someone they love and who will always be their "child." There is hardly a parent support group anywhere that doesn't number among its members people whose self-starving "children" are in their thirties or even forties. This is so largely because these people developed eating disorders years ago, when little was known about them and therapy was practically nonexistent. These are chronic starvers, and they are the most difficult to treat. Although they may be married and have children, their own parents still feel a responsibility to them. It may be—and this is often said in meetings attended by such parents—that truly they can do no more, and should not even try. These comments are nearly always disregarded.

Among the things that parents of a mature starver can and should do are these:

Give the starver all the emotional support possible. Express your love openly and warmly. Grab every opportunity for approval and praise. Try to help her in her efforts at self-identity and independence: do not shove her away, but also do not make it harder for her to gain her release from parental ties. Mothers especially should emphasize the "separateness" of the offspring's life from the mother's, of her identity and the mother's, of their different, individual needs. Make yourself available and make it plain to her that you are available whenever she wants you, not just when you are trying to thrust your help onto her. That help, it should be made clear to her, extends from emotional support to financial assistance with therapy. Make it clear that she will not owe you anything in emotional terms.

Try for trade-offs. It isn't bribery if you say to a child, "Okay, you want to go to college. We're eager to help pay for it. But we feel it would be a waste of your time and our money if you go to college while your problem is unsolved. We want you to get therapy before you enter school or while you are there." If the adult self-starver is living at home and dependent on the parents, or at least accepts room and board from them, it is perfectly appropriate for parents to point out that they are living up to and even beyond their responsibilities by continuing to support her. In turn they could ask her to live up to her responsibilities to herself. This is not meant as a threat and should not sound as if it means "get help or get out." It is simply confronting her with an important reality and asking her to match the family's contribution to her well-being with a contribution of her own on her own behalf.

Unfortunately, there are cases where the emotional destruction suffered by the parents from years of fruitlessly trying to help someone who refuses to be helped can reach the limits of tolerance. At this point parents do indeed tell an adult daughter either to do something about her problem or move out. In fact, this is sometimes effective in making the starver realize she must fix up her life. Other times, however, it only results in a serious rupture between the starver and her family that is never healed. It is impossible to predict the results. In any case, actually "throwing out" your own child is such a serious step it should not be undertaken without outside advice.

It should be emphasized that trade-offs are not bribery but a sharing of responsibilities and an acceptance of the give-and-take of life. Your child should accept your conditions and give you something in return for something you give. Only when they are too young to handle any responsibility should children be "takers" only and not "givers" as well.

While the first concern is to get help for the child who suffers an eating disorder, parents should seriously consider help for themselves, too. The emotional and physical toll on parents can be great. Furthermore, the complexity of the condition, the frustrations inherent in trying to deal with it, and the conflicting advice parents may read or hear from friends can be hopelessly bewildering. Parents, or the parent who shoulders the larger burden, may not need therapy as often or as intensely as the starver does. But an occasional visit to provide emotional support, to clarify muddled or confused thinking, to get advice on specific issues, can be sanity-saving for parents—and helpful for the child's progress as well. The need for a parent to have individual therapy is generally not met by a family therapy program in which parents also attend sessions, because the focus there is specifically on the child's problems. Such sessions may even be stressful for parents. A parental consultation with a therapist is also indicated if you are failing in your effort to get your child into counseling. A skilled professional may be able to devise a method that works for your child.

It should be noted that sometimes, without knowing or intending it, parents themselves may be impediments to getting a child into therapy. Therapists in the student health service at the University of California, Santa Barbara, concerned about self-starving patients who thought they looked "fine" in spite of their obvious emaciation, undertook a survey of the attitudes of families and friends of these patients. The results surprised them. Everyone who responded to the survey expressed concern about the starver's situation, and most were frustrated or angry that she had evaded or defeated their attempts to help. Most also realized that their concern pleased the starver. Both parents and boyfriends were "keenly aware" of starvers' peculiar eating and exercise habits, including gorging and vomiting. Some were embarrassed and found these habits unpleasant. However, all were "astonishingly tolerant." Significantly, the survey revealed that starvers met with more approval than disapproval from family and friends. In a typical case, seven people surveyed described the starver as "slender," ten described her as "neat," and all agreed she was "well groomed" and "fashionable." The words skinny, emaciated, haggard, and abnormal were each mentioned only once. Several of the seven envied the starver's self-control and discipline and one person described the starver as "victorious."

Several starvers in this group admitted to their therapists that they used their condition—or were even encouraged to use it—to gain rewards. For example, one patient was told by her father while on a European trip that if she remained slender he would take her to Europe again rather than her mother, who he said was "putting on a little weight."

Such conditions may counteract professed wishes among parents and friends to help the starver, and if she is getting therapy, "it is not likely to be effective if there are constant reinforcements from family and friends indicating that the patient is attractive, socially accepted and even admired," the California therapists said.[1]

One expert has said that parents who contribute to a delay in getting therapy fall into three groups, which may overlap. The first group consists of parents who do not recognize how serious the condition is. Parents may be self-absorbed and exhausted by work or other responsibilities and may simply not see the gradual change in their child's behavior or feelings. Many parents may even share the values that have driven a starver to this solution to her problem; they may have strong feelings about the importance of personal appearance and may applaud slimness. Academic success and popularity may also be important to them, so if the child is still performing well in school and continues to have an active social life, these signs of success may overshadow their impression of her distress. Sometimes, if either or both parents were especially concerned with weight during their own adolescence, they assume she is going through a normal phase and will soon outgrow it.

The second group of parents are those who do recognize that there is a problem but choose not to intervene because they are afraid their interference will make matters worse, or result in serious rebellion. They may be frightened that focusing attention on the problem or "making too much of it" will change a temporary aberration into a major battleground, making the starver more stubborn and defiant than ever. The child may already be going through some minor, natural rebellion, and the parents may not want to give her reason to be more rebellious. They may fear that making an issue out of the eating problem will fracture an already fragile relationship. They may want to avoid further deterioration of communication that could lead to the "I'll never speak to you again" response.

Sometimes the decision not to intervene comes out of a tacit understanding between the parents that they really do not agree on how to approach the child or handle her. They do not want to confront this difference directly because of the harm it might do their own relationship. Children, especially those with eating disorders, are quick to recognize the signs of such split opinions in their parents, and may play one parent against the other so as to prevent organized intervention.

The third group of parents are those who try to intervene without professional help. They try to do it on their own, collecting much information about eating disorders and applying what they have learned in attempts at do-it-yourself therapy. One reason for this may be that the parents think that seeking professional help would be evidence of their own inadequacies as parents. They also may anticipate that the therapist will blame them for their child's problem or scold them for waiting so long before seeking help. Some may be unconsciously afraid that therapy will unearth other problems in the family or in the marriage, perhaps some guilty secret such as drug or alcohol abuse or infidelity.[2]

It is important for parents who are not actively seeking help for their child to undergo some self-examination to see if they recognize themselves in any of the preceding descriptions. This recognition alone may allow them to overcome obstacles to seeking professional help.

It may reassure parents in this last category to know that experienced and reliable therapists do not take a blaming stance. They usually assume that the family has done and is doing the best they can for their child. Therapists also understand that a family's best is never good enough in the circumstances of eating disorders. Working with such problems is what therapists are for. The family's inability to solve the child's problem on its own should not be regarded as a failure but as an inevitability.

NINE

AFTERWORD: A THERAPIST'S VIEW

BY BERNARD MACKLER, PH.D.

The reasons people become emotionally disturbed are not easy to discern and eating disorders are no exception. We can assume that many underlying forces contribute. These include the drive for perfection, a need to control, pressure to succeed, the desire to look "super," fear of growing up, and the inability to deal with failure. All of these things speak to the person with an eating disorder in frustrating, seemingly overpowering, inner voices.

Both internal and external forces—family, boyfriend, work, school, and society—act in a powerful fashion to undermine confidence. The result is a need for total control. This is obviously unattainable; hence, the victim of an eating disorder is in a trap. Such a person cannot figure out how to live with past failures and imperfections, nor can she learn to live *now* with an eating disorder. Either way, she loses; her lack of confidence forces her into choosing a habit that solves the problem of how to exist but it ironically leads to a life that precludes being and meaning. In the end, it is more than a no-win situation: it is an addiction to a demonic way of existing that leads to a self-serving, egocentric mode of behavior. Such a person lives alone with only her terrors and the meager armor of thinness. The voices of self-hate are quieted, but only temporarily, and she feels no growth, love, or life.

Anorexia nervosa and bulimia are not easily defined. We can say, however, that in anorexia there is a person who wants to starve herself. This disorder is quite apparent even to the non-specialist. In bulimia, all the covert binging, vomiting, laxatives, suppositories, and other clandestine food-ridding behaviors are less apparent to others. The person usually appears normal, at least physically.

Most of us are appalled that these gross disorders occur in otherwise apparently ordinary people. Some suggest that there is some biogenetic and physiological basis. Others accept the fact that the disorders are psychological and try to explain them as forms of petty malingering, exaggerated egocentrism, or bizarre pathological processes. We could, however, very reasonably call eating disorders inefficient and unhealthy, immature ways of solving problems that are common to us all.

A WAY OUT

There is a positive route and direction for the suffering. Since the major cause of a person's inability to live a full life is misdirected emotion, it would seem plausible that a psychological remedy is in order. If people who were insensitive caused the problem, people who are hopeful, thoughtful, firm, and reasonable can and do bring about a new life. Hope, provided realistically, is the major ingredient to improvement. A frightened person mentally bent on order, who feels that life is hopeless, needs a new and smiling person to help her struggle out of the labyrinth of despair. This person need not be a psychologist or psychotherapist. In our society, however, a professional is the most likely person to help because he has the experience that makes him capable of understanding what is happening in the inner soul of these traumatized and anxiety-driven sufferers.

TYRANNY

Often I hear that these sufferers are tyrants. Parents and friends perceive them as always dictating to others, particularly parents. This is often also the way sufferers perceive themselves.

They are dictatorial, because they know how to push weak people around. In their struggle to control their emotional turmoil they learn how to control others and need to do so, since they cannot control themselves. But are they really tyrants? The live in fear. They constantly hate themselves, either because their parents were ineffectual or contemptuous or because they feel in a moralistic way that they want to be very good daughters and think they know better than their parents how to achieve this.

Tyrants do abuse others, and people with eating disorders can be abusive, but unlike true dictators, these people also inflict much pain upon themselves. They cannot live with themselves or with anyone else. When they finally get thoroughly fed up with themselves, the few people who still care for them become scapegoats of their immature feelings.

The real tyrant is not the person but the fear that overwhelms her. Such people have not had the courage nor the ability to deal with overwhelming anxiety. They have not learned self-mastery and so they run away from their fears, leaving themselves vulnerable to more pain and more tyranny from fear. Because they do not know how to confront and conquer their fears, they are constantly at the mercy of their fears. Eventually they come to feel that death or total mental paralysis will be the inevitable result.

How does one get to understand people so afflicted? Professionals and nonprofessionals alike are shocked by this strange new behavior and they are at a loss how to cope with it, how to change the situation, how to pull the victim out of the quicksand of her disorder.

I am not fond of theorizing but I do have to use concepts, otherwise I would not be able to use language, treat patients, or even write this chapter. So I will speak of the concept of "maturity" as having some importance in understanding or dealing with anorexia and bulimia. (Therapists and parents often tell me which disorder, anorexia or bulimia, is "worse" or hardest to treat. Patients never ask me; they are only concerned with their own problems.) I have seen people with anorexia who are more mature than patients with bulimia. Usually, however, I believe bulimics are more "mature," because they more often work, relate to others, and have an active—although empty—sex life. Anorexia forecloses relationships with others. Responsible and sometimes even excessive work may occur among anorectics, but sex is out.

Time is another important concept. For these people, the future is frightening because unknowns reside there. Life is filled with the unexpected; if you are terrified of what might happen, if the unexpected fills you with fear because you cannot control it, the future is to be avoided. A sensitive soul who has been hurt, after all, does not want to live a life where hurt could happen again; the past proves that life is always negative.

The past thus dominates such people; they live with past hurts and pain. They cannot let go of the past and forgive others or themselves for it. As perfectionists, they assume that life must have no mistakes in it. If pain is inflicted, it is their own fault; they have no self-respect or confidence, so how can they possibly think the pain was caused by another? Feelings are the healthy person's means of living in the present. When one's feelings are confused or distorted, when one is obsessed about the future and regurgitates the past, there is no room for the present. This kind of person does not trust emotions, particularly since they seem uncontrollable and have created friction and confusion in the past. Emotions, the present, life itself are dangerous and must be avoided.

To succeed in recovering, the patient has to be brought into the present. To be sure, the past is with us and so is the future, but the present needs to be pushed to the fore. Too many anorectic and bulimic patients squeeze away their "now." They do not live in the present because they are preoccupied with their doubts about the future and their failures of the past. They are obsessed with these things; they "obsess away" whatever might be happening now, and they obsess away decisions, risks, growth, laughter, love, and hurt.

Obviously, such people cannot function or cope with life's exigencies. To clear away obsessive thinking, the solution is to *do*. These people get involved in nonconstructive actions only. This is their way of dealing with the confusion in their heads and their constant search for a solution that contains no possibility of failure in the future. These acts include magical thinking and ritualistic behavior, such as not eating all day but waiting for the excitement of eating one forbidden fruit or chocolate cookie at night. Strict control over their eating patterns allows them to avoid dealing with a spontaneous moment like running into a friend who might suggest a movie or a slice of pizza. If divided into carefully scheduled periods, each day can be precisely controlled and ordered. Life becomes structured in rituals.

Although therapy is itself scheduled for specific regular times, it can overcome rituals if the therapist is honest, caring, and spontaneous. By freely expressing care and by focusing on sharing the burden, the therapist can lead the patient into giving up her mind games. By making the relationship become real and not part of a controlled game, by helping the patient to accept love, trust, and freedom, the therapist can show the patient that there is a better way to live.

The person with either anorexia or bulimia is reluctant to

reveal or share her mental gymnastics. Her combat thinking is strictly private and off-limits to anyone, especially a nosy therapist. If questioned or interviewed, she will become defiant and bold. An innocent face with sweet honest eyes will look back and yield nothing. Ironically, however, a patient will readily share her mind games if the therapist can first guess what they are. Here persistence and care can eventually overcome fears and cynicism. It is a slow journey, but the goal of finding a new life is worth the effort.

Compulsive rituals differ among anorectics and bulimics. The anorectic may eat alone but everyone knows what she eats. There is no hidden eating, gorging, and getting rid of food as there is with the bulimic. Anorexia, therefore, is the more "honest" eating disorder. For that matter, so is excessive obesity. Everyone can see that the person is unhealthy. We may not be able to tell why or how, but we know it to be the case.

In bulimia the behavior is less overt. Why be honest if you cannot be, or if you will be severely reprimanded?

Both kinds of behavior are baffling and both are life-threatening. Anorexia is more frightening, especially to parents, because the sufferer can become positively skeletal. Bulimia is not so obviously dangerous, but this is deceiving. Bulimia can also kill. One great danger of this is that bulimics cannot be trusted to respond to warnings that binging and purging can destroy the teeth or cause fatal heart attacks through dehydration and chemical imbalances.

Once, during a first session with an extremely bulimic patient, I was shocked to discover that she was taking lithium (a drug used to treat the manic phase of manic-depression), which can exaggerate and complicate the chemical problems of bulimia. I immediately called the physician who had prescribed the drug to tell him of the dangers. He replied that he was well aware of the bulimia and of the possible harmful effects of lithium combined with vomiting, but said it was all right because he had spoken to the patient. "I told her not to vomit," he said.

What he and others who are inexperienced with this disorder do not realize is that bulimics lie. They may report that they are not vomiting even if they are, and even if the evidence is fairly obvious. But these people are so committed to lying and deceit that they begin to believe their own fantasies.

SUICIDE AND DEATH

Anorexia and bulimia are life-impairing difficulties. They can also be life-threatening. People with these disorders must be taken seriously; family and therapists must be vigilant and take heed when the victim is too tired to work or study and talks about walking in front of a car or swallowing a bottle of pills. The need for control looms so large in these people's minds that when control lapses, life becomes madness. For the person suffering a profound eating disorder, life is all about having everything in the right place; their weight, their studies, the person or people they care about, their room and their clothes. If one or more of these points goes out of control, such a person might decide, "Why bother?"

There is an important difference between obsessively playing with the idea of suicide and a genuine decision or attempt to do so. Family members and therapists must be sensitive to the nuances, but if they cannot judge with certainty, they must assume that every precaution is necessary.

Fortunately, it is possible to break endless obsession with death by showing the victim of an eating disorder that this is just one of many obsessions—that she obsesses, period. This realization can bring her a great sense of relief and free her energies for more healthy activities.

It is a great risk for a therapist or parent to assume that when a person cuts her wrists it is not a real suicide attempt. It is true, however, that such a person usually just wants a firm and caring reaction from family or other loved ones. Anorexics and bulimics are not used to genuine concern and anger; they are more used to irrational outbursts from frustrated parents about manners, money, or a clean room. When parents genuinely express the feeling that they want their child to live, that her death would hurt them deeply, that her self-destruction would make them angry because they would miss her, they communicate genuine care and love. This is not a "technique" for averting suicide; it is a genuine expression of emotions, which such people need desperately.

THERAPY AND THERAPISTS

Many psychotherapists are either afraid to work with such complicated people or, if willing, are untrained and ill-equipped. These patients are taking tremendous risks in trusting themselves to a therapist; the therapist must be willing to take risks as well. He is on the spot: he must make decisions not only for himself but for his patient, because until she begins to recover, she is incapable of making them for herself. Direct intervention, however, goes absolutely against a therapist's training. He has been taught to listen and understand, but *never* to make value judgments, to act for or decide for another person.

The therapist must be on firm ground, for he may be tested at any moment. Honesty, openness, trust, the meaning of life—all sorts of serious questions will come under close scrutiny. The therapist must respond to the questions, prove his honesty, reaffirm his openness, repeat his answers many times, and all without losing patience. He also must be prepared to be a model, a decision-maker, a caretaker, and most of all, must be ready and willing to help people who are very frightened indeed. Without actually being a father, lover, or friend, he must be a parenting figure, loving, and involved—all the while still remaining a professional. These are paradoxical issues therapists must face and resolve early in their careers if they are to help these terrified and insecure girls and young women with eating disorders.

For parents, as for therapists, feeling a child's anxieties requires a good firm memory that is in touch with those times when you were confronted with terrible doubt, or indecision. Only then can you see the commonality between yourself and your child. Understanding, being with your child, and caring for your child in the immediate present is difficult when you are preoccupied with your own needs and what you want and need to do.

WHO KNOWS WHY THEY DO IT?

Children with eating disorders are not crazy, weird, or absurd. They are not to be despised. They are human beings like you and me, with feelings and interesting ideas: in fact, they run the gamut of behavior and personality. Each child, therefore, has to be helped and understood on her own terms without any strict rules that might guide or confuse you.

Certainly eating disorders are the fad of the eighties. Every generation seems to have one notable diagnostic category that everyone is both appalled by and curious about. Every generation also has a problem category of people who have real difficulty in maturing, and our society has many such people. People with eating disorders, however, have no monopoly in this respect; it is simply that these people's immaturity and fears focus on food and weight. But do not be blinded into believing that society is totally to blame. Vanity has been with us for a long time and focusing on weight or appearance is not new. On the whole, people are not very creative. We choose our mental problems partly on our own, but always along the lines suggested by society. Evidence of our conforming behavior is everywhere: alcohol and drugs have twenty to forty million devotees. Some twenty million people jog.

Nevertheless, we should all avoid the pitfall of seeing all eating-disordered people as the same. Each person is unique. Your child's uniqueness is something precious for you to love and reward, and for her to finally recognize as being valuable.

TEN

ALL KINDS OF HELP

Regardless of what parents may do to help their self-starving child back to normal life, they need all the help they can get to cope and survive—and this definitely includes help for themselves. Individual therapy for one or both parents can be remarkably beneficial. Whether or not parents are receiving such help, but especially if they are not, the greatest source of information, comfort, and encouragement can be found in parent support groups. Depending on the organization, these group meetings may include professional and formal presentations, workshops, and informal talk sessions. The latter allow parents to describe their problems and experiences and learn valuable lessons from other people's experience. These groups also provide considerable consolation and encouragement by revealing to parents that they are not alone in their suffering, and also that good outcomes do occur. Many parents, out of a wish to help others and because of the close friendships that often evolve in such groups, continue to attend after their own children have recovered. These parents can be a rich source of advice and experience as well as a reminder that the suffering does end and life does get back to normal. Perhaps equally important is that such groups reveal the great variety of personalities, child-rearing practices, and backgrounds of self-starvers' families. Parents can see that the other participants are not all "bad" parents who have "failed" in their parental tasks and thus produced a self-starver. This realization is a great guilt reliever. So is the discovery that whatever bizarre and terrible things are happening in your family have happened before and are happening still in millions of other families. You are not uniquely victimized.

There are also self-help groups for the self-starver and binge/purger. Groups for the latter, however, seem to be more successful. Many self-starvers are reluctant to attend such meetings because they are afraid they will not be the thinnest girl in the room. In fact, some girls have been set back by attending such meetings because they were not the thinnest girl in the room. This immediately prompted them to exert greater efforts at dieting. Parents might be wise to provide information about such groups to their child and to encourage her and support her if she expresses a wish to attend, but should not pressure her to do so.

Information about support groups may be found in the local telephone directory, local newspapers, public libraries, hospitals, medical schools, city or county social service departments or self-help hotlines, and school guidance counselors. Below is a list of a number of national organizations that provide information about support groups along with other kinds of information and referrals to therapists.

NATIONAL ORGANIZATIONS

American Anorexia Nervosa Association, Inc., 133 Cedar Lane, Teaneck, N.J. 07666. Offers information, referrals, counseling, self-help groups, a speakers' bureau, and research. Publishes five newsletters a year and holds five general meetings a year that are open to the public. These feature professional presentations or workshops. Sponsors monthly self-help sessions for starvers and bingers led by recovered victims, parents, and professionals. Arranges for written or telephone contact with recovered victims. Telephone (201) 836-1800 between 10 A.M. and 2 P.M. (EST) weekdays.

Anorexia Bulimia Care, Inc., Box 213, Lincoln Center, MA 01773. Services similar to above. In addition, this group has training workshops for people who wish to become "facilitators," or leaders, of support groups.

Bulimia Anorexia Self Help, 621 S. New Ballas, Suite 6005, Tower B., St. Louis, MO 63141. Services similar to above. Also has training programs for facilitators.

Anorexia Nervosa and Related Eating Disorders, Inc., P.O. Box 5102, Eugene, OR 97405. Provides information and support similar to above groups as well as a twenty-four-hour hotline: (503) 344-1144.

National Anorexia Aid Society, P.O. Box 29461, Columbus, OH 43229. Has support groups in many states and a national referral system. Nominal membership fee includes four newsletters yearly.

National Association of Anorexia and Associated Disorders, Inc., Box 271, Highland Park, IL 60035. The first such national association, it provides national referrals, self-help groups, early detection and prevention programs, and a large package of information on request. Has twenty-four-hour hotline: (312) 831-3438. This organization is particularly active and vigorous in helping form chapters and local self-help groups and giving them continued assistance.

The Center for the Study of Anorexia and Bulimia of the Institute for Contemporary Psychotherapy, One West

91st St., New York, NY 10024. The Center holds meetings and symposia of national interest and provides information on prevention and early detection as well as pamphlets on eating disorders. The Center offers individual and/or family therapy with sliding-scale fees. It is also a leader in the training of new therapists and holds workshops and symposia for professionals that are also open (for a fee) to nonprofessionals.

Most of these organizations have nominal fees or none. They are often supported entirely by donations or by a variety of charitable events such as antique fairs. When writing for information, send a self-addressed stamped envelope.

For children with eating disorders who are having trouble attending school or keeping up with their work, there are several sources of help. In some states, a child with an eating disorder can be classified as handicapped, thus qualifying her for free tutoring supported by state aid. School guidance counselors or psychologists can assist and provide information on such programs.

In addition, those who cannot attend school regularly or who need to catch up on work, may be able to do so though the National University Continuing Education Association, which coordinates independent guided study courses (by correspondence) for credit through individual colleges and universities. These courses are at both the high school and college levels. They are provided by highly reputable and accredited American schools, thus credits earned through the program are widely accepted by other schools and colleges. In some courses, all assignments including final examinations are conducted entirely by mail. Other courses require the student to take a final examination and/or several interim examinations, but the student may arrange to take these at a nearby local college or with a qualified proctor.

These are not commercial, mail-order style correspondence courses of dubious quality or value. They can, in fact, be highly demanding, since the student is essentially working alone and must exert self-discipline and self-motivation. However, girls with eating disorders who have undergone such study have reported that the completion of the work "all on their own" gave them a great sense of accomplishment and bolstered their sense of self-worth.

Information about courses, requirements, and fees can be found in *The Independent Study Catalogue.* It may be available at school or public libraries, or can be ordered from: NUCEA Book Order Department, Peterson's Guides, P.O. Box 2123, Princeton, NJ 08540. As of this writing, the price is $5.95 plus $1.25 postage and handling.

HOSPITAL-ASSOCIATED PROGRAMS

Alabama
Department of Psychiatry
  School of Medicine
  Birmingham, AL 35294

District of Columbia
Department of Psychiatry
  Children's Hospital—
  National Medical Center
  111 Michigan Ave
  Washington, D.C. 20010

Illinois
Eating Disorders Program
  Michael Reese Hospital
  29th St and Ellis Ave
  Chicago, IL 60616

Eating Disorders Program
  Northwestern Memorial
  Hospital
  320 East Huron
  Chicago, IL 60611

HELP (Health, Eating and
Lifestyle Program)
  Forest Hospital
  555 Wilson Lane
  Des Plaines, IL 60016

Maryland
National Institute of Mental
  Health
  Clinical Center Building
  9000 Rockville Pike
  Bethesda, MD 20014

Massachusetts
Mailman Research Center
  McLean Hospital
  115 Mill Street
  Belmont, MA 02178

Department of Psychiatry
  Children's Hospital Medical
  Center
  300 Longwood Ave
  Boston, MA 02115

Eating Disorders Unit
Massachusetts General
Hospital
Fruit Street
Boston, MA 02114

Minnesota

Department of Psychiatry
University Hospital
Box 393 Mayo Memorial
Building
420 Delaware St S.E.
Minneapolis, MN 55455

Section of Child and
Adolescent Psychiatry
Mayo Clinic
200 First St S.W.
Rochester, MN 55905

Missouri

Anorexia Bulimia Treatment
and Education Center
St. John's Mercy Medical
Center
615 South New Ballas Road
St. Louis, MO 63141

New York

Department of Psychiatry
Montefiore Hospital and
Medical Center
111 East 210th St
Bronx, NY 10466

Columbia Center for Eating
Disorders
Columbia-Presbyterian
Medical Center
38 East 61st St
New York, NY 10021

Four Winds Hospital
Cross River and Route 35
Katonah, NY 10536

Eating Disorders Program
St. Vincent's Hospital
Harrison, NY 10528

North Carolina

Anorexia Nervosa Treatment
Program
Box 3125
Duke University Medical
Center
Durham, NC 27110

Ohio

Eating Disorders Clinic
Psychiatry Department
University of Cincinnati
Medical Center
Cincinnati, OH 45221

Section of Child and
Adolescent Psychiatry
Cleveland Clinic Foundation
9500 Euclid Ave
Cleveland, OH 44106

Pennsylvania

Philadelphia Child Guidance
Clinic
34th and Civic Center
Boulevard
Philadelphia, PA 19104

Center for Behavioral Medicine
Box 495
Hospital of the University of
Pennsylvania
3400 Spruce Street
Philadelphia, PA 19104

Texas
Department of Psychiatry
  Baylor College of Medicine
  Houston Medical Center
  1200 Moursund Ave
  Houston, TX 77030

Wisconsin
Center for Eating Disorders
  30 South Henry Street
  P.O. Box 8678
  Madison, WI 53708

FURTHER READING

As recently as five or six years ago, there was literally only one book on eating disorders that could be of any help to parents: Hilde Bruch's *The Golden Cage* and perhaps the novel, *The Best Little Girl in the World*. Since 1979 or 1980, dozens of books have appeared either specifically intended for the nonscientific public or written in language that the nonscientist can understand. A selection of these books follows. Asterisks indicate a preference of the author for this book.

A word of caution should be said. Even some of the best of these books may make parents uneasy because of emphasis on "what's wrong with the family." When encountering such material, parents should constantly remind themselves of several things. First, *all parents,* not just those of children with eating disorders, have their faults. They are all human. Family living is full of potential for conflict and wrong judgments. Parents who have children without eating disorders may have—usually do have—children with other problems, some even more serious. Second, some families with the same problems as yours may not have children with eating disorders. There is no clearcut, direct, inevitable connection between a particular problem in a family and the development of an eating disorder. The presence of over-protective mothers or negligent fathers does not necessarily mean there will be a child who starves herself.

There is one further problem with this additional reading. Many parents find it extremely frustrating to read highly detailed case histories. A case history may include some features that are pertinent to your child's situation, but it will inevitably differ in many ways. No case history will exactly parallel your child's; therefore, do not expect case histories to provide you with an instant understanding of your child's problem or any magic solution to it.

*Boskind-White, Marlene, and White, William C., Jr. *Bulimarexia, the Binge/Purge Cycle.* New York: W.W. Norton & Co., 1983.

Bruch, Hilde. *Eating Disorders.* New York: Basic Books, 1973.

*Bruch, Hilde. *The Golden Cage: The Enigma of Anorexia Nervosa.* Cambridge, MA: Harvard University Press, 1978.

Cauwels, Janice M. *Bulimia: The Binge-Purge Compulsion.* New York: Doubleday & Co., 1983.

Chernin, Kim. *The Obsession: Reflections on the Tyranny of Slenderness.* New York: Harper & Row, 1981.

*Crisp, A. H. *Anorexia Nervosa: Let Me Be.* New York: Grune and Stratton, 1980.

Kinoy, Barbara P. *When Will We Laugh Again?* New York: Columbia University Press, 1984.

Landau, Elaine. *Why Are They Starving Themselves? Understanding Anorexia Nervosa and Bulimia.* New York: Brunner/Mazel, 1982.

Levenkron, Steven. *The Best Little Girl in the World.* Chicago: Contemporary Books, 1978.

*Levenkron, Steven. *Treating and Overcoming Anorexia Nervosa.* New York: Charles Scribner's Sons, 1982.

*MacLeod, Sheila. *The Art of Starvation.* New York: Schocken Books, 1982.

Minuchin, Salvatore. *Psychosomatic Families: Anorexia Nervosa in Context.* Cambridge, MA: Harvard University Press, 1978.

Orbach, Suzie. *Fat is a Feminist Issue.* Berkeley, CA: Paddington Press, 1978.

Palazzoli, Maria Selvini. *Self-Starvation*. New York: Jason Aronson, 1978.

Pope, Harrison G., and Hudson, James. *New Hope for Binge Eaters*. New York: Harper & Row, 1984.

Roth, Geneen. *Feeding the Hungry Heart: The Experience of Compulsive Eating*. New York: Bobbs-Merrill Co, Inc., 1983.

Rumney, Avis. *Dying to Please: Anorexia and Its Cure*. Jefferson, NC: MacFarlane, 1982.

Sours, John. *Starving to Death in a Sea of Objects: The Anorexia Nervosa Syndrome*. New York: Jason Aronson, 1980.

Vigersky, Robert. *Anorexia Nervosa*. New York: Raven Press, 1967.

Vincent, L. M. *Competing with the Sylph: Dancers and the Pursuit of the Ideal Body Form*. Andrews & McNeel, Inc., 1979.

Wilson, C. Philip, Hogan, Charles, and Mintz, Lea. *The Fear of Being Fat: The Treatment of Anorexia and Bulimia*. New York: Jason Aronson, 1983.

NOTES

INTRODUCTION

1. Sharon Glick Miller and Henry P. Power, "Support Groups for Eating Disordered Patients," in Pauline Powers and Robert Fernandez (eds.), *Current Treatment of Anorexia Nervosa and Bulimia* (Basel and New York: Karger, 1984), p. 294.

ONE: HOW DID THIS HAPPEN?

1. Jill Welbourne and Joan Purgold, *The Eating Sickness* (Bristol: The Harvester Press, 1984), p. 34.
2. Welbourne and Purgold, p. 35.
3. Maria Selvini Palazzoli, *Self Starvation* (London: Chaucer Publishing Co., 1974), p. 35.
4. John Sours, *Starving to Death in a Sea of Objects* (New York and London: Jason Aronson, 1980), p. 282.
5. Sours, p. 283.
6. A. H. Crisp, Presentation on "Hilde Bruch Day," Columbia University College of Physicians and Surgeons and the New York State Psychiatric Institute, April 18, 1986.
7. Hilde Bruch, *Eating Disorders* (New York: Basic Books, 1973), p. 101.
8. Bruch, p. 101.
9. Welbourne and Purgold, p. 30.
10. Welbourne and Purgold, p. 31.

11. Welbourne and Purgold, p. 33.

12. Welbourne and Purgold, p. 34.

13. Susanne Abraham and Derek Llewellyn-Jones, *Eating Disorders* (Oxford: Oxford University Press, 1984), p. 30.

14. See Note 6.

15. A. H. Crisp, "The Psychopathology of Anorexia Nervosa: Getting the 'Heat' Out of the System" in Albert J. Stunkard and Eliot Steller, *Eating and Its Disorders* (New York: Raven Press, 1984), p. 209.

Two: The Terror and the Tyranny

1. A. H. Crisp, "The Psychopathology of Anorexia Nervosa: Getting the 'Heat' Out of the System" in Albert J. Stunkard and Eliot Steller, *Eating and Its Disorders* (New York: Raven Press, 1984), p. 211.

2. Pauline Powers, *Current Treatment of Anorexia Nervosa and Bulimia* (Basel, New York: S. Karger 1984), p. 19.

3. Hilde Bruch, *The Golden Cage* (Cambridge, Mass.: Harvard University Press, 1978), p. 8.

4. Bruch, p. 11.

5. Powers, p. 25.

6. Powers, p. 134.

7. May Wazeter, "Alive Again," *YM Magazine*, June/July 1984, p. 52.

8. Bruch, p. 116.

9. Jill Welbourne and Joan Purgold, *The Eating Sickness* (Bristol: The Harvester Press, 1984), p. 55.

10. Welbourne and Purgold, p. 55.

Three: The Special Problems of the Binge Eater

1. Jill Welbourne and Joan Purgold, *The Eating Sickness* (Bristol: The Harvester Press, 1984), p. 34.

2. Arnold Anderson, *Practical Comprehensive Treatment of An-*

orexia Nervosa and Bulimia (Baltimore, Md.: The Johns Hopkins Press, 1985), p. 109.

3. Anderson, p. 110.

4. Anderson, p. 109.

5. C. L. Fairburn and P. J. Cooper, "The Clinical Features of Bulimia Nervosa," *British Journal of Psychiatry* 141:238–246.

6. Welbourne and Purgold, p. 71.

7. Welbourne and Purgold, p. 72.

8. Welbourne and Purgold, p. 72.

9. Welbourne and Purgold, p. 63.

10. Welbourne and Purgold, p. 64.

11. Welbourne and Purgold, p. 65.

12. Welbourne and Purgold, p. 65.

13. Welbourne and Purgold, p. 71.

14. Marlene Boskind-White and William C. White, Jr., *Bulimarexia, the Binge/Purge Cycle* (New York: W. W. Norton & Co., 1983), p. 67.

15. Boskind-White, p. 69.

16. Boskind-White, p. 159.

17. Joel Yager, "The Treatment of Bulimia: An Overview," in Pauline Powers and Robert C. Fernandez (eds.), *Current Treatment of Anorexia Nervosa and Bulimia* (Basel and New York: Karger, 1984), p. 63.

18. Anderson, p. 123.

19. Yager, p. 68.

20. Boskind-White, p. 161.

21. Boskind-White, p. 203.

22. Fairburn and Cooper, p. 241.

FOUR: COPING DAY BY DAY

1. Barbara Kinoy, *When Will We Laugh Again?* (New York: Columbia University Press, 1984), p. 97.

2. Steven Levenkron, *Treating and Overcoming Anorexia Nervosa* (New York: Charles Scribner's Sons, 1982), p. 189.

3. Jill Welbourne and Joan Purgold, *The Eating Sickness* (Bristol: The Harvester Press, 1984), p. 42.

Six: Father: The Most Important Man

1.   Bernd Huebeck, Johanna Watson and Graeme Russell, "Father Involvement and Responsibility in Family Therapy" in Michael Lamb (ed.), *The Father's Role: Applied Perspective* (New York: John Wiley and Sons, 1986), p. 191.

2.   Graeme Russell, *The Changing Role of Fathers?* (Queensland, Australia: University of Queensland Press, 1983), p. 100.

3.   Graeme Russell, p. 101.

4.   Michael Lamb, *The Role of the Father in Child Development* (New York: John Wiley and Sons, 1976), p. 1.

5.   Henry Biller, *Father, Child and Sex Role* (Lexington, MA: D. D. Heath and Company, 1971), p. 109.

6.   Biller, p. 109.

7.   Graeme Russell, p. 180.

8.   Steven Levenkron, *Treating and Overcoming Anorexia Nervosa* (New York: Charles Scribner's Sons, 1982), p. 3.

9.   Margo Maine, "Engaging the Disengaged Father in the Treatment of Eating Disordered Adolescents." Presented at the Fourth Annual Conference sponsored by the Center for the Study of Anorexia Nervosa and Bulimia, Nov. 16–17, 1985, New York, p. 1.

10.   Maine, p. 4.

11.   Maine, p. 11.

12.   Maine, p. 5.

13.   Marlene Boskind-White and William C. White, Jr., *Bulimarexia: the Binge-Purge Cycle* (New York: W. W. Norton & Co., 1983), p. 74.

14.   Maine, p. 10.

15.   Russell, p. 98.

16.   Maine, p. 6.

Seven: Goals and Types of Therapy

1.   Hilde Bruch, "Psychotherapy in Anorexia Nervosa and Developmental Obesity" in Richard K. Goodstein (ed.), New York: Springer Publishing Company, 1983, p. 138.

2.   Bruch, p. 138.

3.   Hilde Bruch, *Eating Disorders* (New York: Basic Books, Inc., 1973), p. 336.

4.   Bruch, p. 337.

5.   A. H. Crisp, "Treatment and Outcome in Anorexia Nervosa" in Richard K. Goodstein (ed.), *Eating and Weight Disorders* (New York: Springer Publishing Company, 1983), p. 96.

EIGHT: THERAPY: GETTING THERE IS HALF THE BATTLE

1.   C. H. Branch, Hardin and Linda Euman, "Social Attitudes toward Patients with Anorexia Nervosa," *American Journal of Psychiatry* (May 1980), 137:5, 631–2.

2.   Arnold E. Anderson, *Practical Comprehensive Treatment of Anorexia Nervosa and Bulimia* (Baltimore: The Johns Hopkins University Press, 1985), p. 98.

INDEX